BACKFIRE
IN
NEPAL

BACKFIRE IN NEPAL

how INDIA LOST THE PLOT TO CHINA

SANJAY UPADHYA

Vitasta

LET KNOWLEDGE SPREAD

Published by
Renu Kaul Verma
Vitasta Publishing Pvt Ltd
2/15, Ansari Road, Daryaganj
New Delhi-110 002
info@vitastapublishing.com

ISBN 978-81-948200-2-4
© Sanjay Upadhya
First Edition 2021

MRP ₹495

Editor: Kanishk Shekhar
Cover: Somesh Kumar Mishra
Layout: Vits Press
Printed by Chaman Enterprises, New Delhi

For Ranu, Jay and Nilu

Contents

Preface

Working on this book has been a satisfying learning experience, one of revisiting accepted wisdom, retracing steps and looking for missed signs. After India drove an ambitious agenda for change in Nepal in 2006, my attention instantly shifted to China, whose role in the country has been unconventional, to say the least. China must have felt doubly aggrieved. Its traditional ally, the monarchy, was pushed towards eventual oblivion; until the very end, China had armed the palace to fight the now-ascendant Maoist rebels. But, then, unsentimental pragmatism had driven China to shed all ideological shibboleths while dealing with Nepal. Since the founding of the People's Republic in 1949, Beijing had established itself as the quintessential practitioner of the attribute in domestic and international affairs. Unlike in the aftermath of the political changes of 1990 in Nepal, China was poised for proactivity. Could it contend with the emphatic gains India and West had just made?

There were abundant cautionary clues. India's effort was at best tentative, as it had to manage competing domestic and international interests. Still, my first book on the subject (The Raj Lives, 2008) was unequivocal in its assertion. Four years later, my second book (Nepal and the Geo-strategic Rivalry Between China and India, 2012) chronicled a competition far benign from what it has become. By 2020, India would lose the plot to China through a combination of events and approaches the COVID-19 pandemic only had exacerbated.

The story is still unfolding, but there is enough material for an informed exploration of the personalities, perspectives and prescriptions that prolonged what was always going to be a turbulent transition. Nepal had to weigh its authentic national aspirations against the real and perceived insecurities of its two giant neighbours. Countries and organisations with deeper pockets but shorter attention spans were the most generous in suggestions. They often defined peace and stability narrowly, both individually and in terms of issues. Popular as some elements of the Western agenda were, they often alienated India or China – and both, at times. As the transition dragged on, India lost ground in traditional constituencies and China expanded into new ones. For Nepal's political players – old and new ones alike – the peace process became an exercise in improvisation. Every twist and turn was as vital as the substance and sequence of the movement.

The best way to convey a coherent narrative, I feel, is to break down the past decade and a half (2005-2020) into what I considered were the key phases. The following chapters move chronologically, beginning with the fall of the monarchy and ascent of the Maoists, to the provisional parliament, the failure of the first constituent assembly to write a new Constitution, the rush job by the second, the three-tier elections, and, finally, the post-election communist majority government. The last chapter peers into the future, taking a more in-depth look into the past and present.

Relying heavily on my earlier works, I have also borrowed extensively from many others who have been closely monitoring the undulations from their respective perches within Nepal and outside. Personal conversations and online communications with many of the people integrally involved throughout this process have been illuminating. The passions and politics of particular moments obfuscate what is already a complicated story. The reticence and reserve of the players on critical issues only obscure things. I have attempted to reflect the views of others accurately. The rest of the assumptions and assertions come from my research and reflections. The author's predispositions and predilections are bound to appear in many places and in manifold forms. All errors of fact are my own.

I want to express my gratitude to Renu Kaul Verma of Vitasta Publishing for her constant encouragement. Every time something threw me into a rant at home, Ranu, my better half, advised that these extended monologues were better suited for another book. Her continued exhortations were evidence of her sincerity. Son Jay and daughter Nilu sacrificed so much time that belonged to them. Without the patience, understanding and encouragement of people too many to name, this book would have been impossible. Thank you, everybody.

—Sanjay Upadhya
Winter Springs, Florida
2020

Introduction

THE IRONY COULD not have been unkinder. In 2005, India facilitates an ambitious alliance between mainstream Nepalese opposition parties agitating against the monarchy and Maoist rebels waging a bloody decade-long insurgency against both parliament and the palace. Driven by a desire to restore democracy from an increasingly audacious king, India has an unspoken objective: to pull Nepal away from the dangerous tilt it sees the palace taking towards China. Beijing, which helped the monarchy fight the Maoists until the very end, becomes the ultimate beneficiary of New Delhi's success.

A decade and a half later, Nepal-India relations – incessantly touted as unparalleled in the world for their depth and diversity – hit their nadir. Graduating from their trademark rhetoric against India, the unified Maoist and Marxist-Leninist factions running the government prepare a new political map incorporating territory Nepal insists India has been illegally occupying for decades. Before India can react coherently, the

Nepalese government amends the Constitution to include the new map as part of the national emblem with overwhelming cross-party support. Traditional friends of India such as the Nepali Congress and Madhes-based parties back Prime Minister Khadga Prasad Sharma Oli's government for its courageous stand on nationalism. The sole legislator who counsels reason is expelled from the body for being a naturalised citizen and, worse, having spoken in Hindi. She forgot that former Indians must have left their language at the border.

Emboldened by the nationwide fervour, Oli's official pronouncements turn eerily outlandish, even for someone known for employing earthy banter to convey urgent matters of state. During a key annual speech in parliament, the prime minister asserts the strain of the coronavirus entering Nepal from India is more virulent than the one that originated in China. Weeks later, he publicly accuses New Delhi of instigating rivals to oust him from power. Then an officially atheist Oli maintains that Lord Ram was born in Nepal, not Ayodhya, before accusing India of cultural encroachment.

Cartography, coup rumours and culture mesh into an even more explosive mix. The ruling Nepal Communist Party (NCP) enjoys close to a two-thirds majority in parliament. Yet it is riven with deep factionalism rooted in personal ambitions and the conflicting schooling of the Maoists and Marxist-Leninists factions. The Chinese ambassador scurries from the residence of one communist leader to another to prevent an impending party split. Those scenes are reminiscent of what generations of Indian ambassadors were castigated for doing. But they are of no solace to New Delhi. A leading member of the Oli cabinet defends China's positive intervention in contrast to India's long record of negative meddling. India is left agog at Oli's audacity, but more so at the inroads the Chinese must have made to encourage it. The stakes rise with New Delhi and Beijing embroiled in their worst border clashes since the 1962 war.

And the monarch ousted for his pro-Chinese tilt? Citizen Gyanendra Shah effectively remains the unofficial head of state, issuing messages on national occasions and exhorting his successors not to upset the precarious balance his ancestors struck between the Asian giants to maintain Nepal's independence. As more and more people seem to want the king's official reinstatement to ensure national stability, he seems to relish the role of chief comforter. The crown does not seem to hold the same attraction. Still, India and – and far less conspicuously – China continue engaging with him as a key national stakeholder.

What happened then? Most analysts – including this author – believed New Delhi had adroitly regained the initiative in Nepal. Supporters and critics of India's role alike were awed by how India pulled off the near-impossible. New Delhi brought together opposing Nepalese political forces on a new national course, mindful of ensuring that India's interests prevailed. Most importantly, it accomplished the task by winning the approval of a populace traditionally sceptical of their southern neighbour.

Officially, China was not the cause – and need not have been – for the change. The democracy defence is eternally effective. The Nepalese monarch's proclamation dismissing the coalition government led by the Nepali Congress' Prime Minister Sher Bahadur Deuba mirrored the words his father, King Mahendra, had used 45 years earlier to dismiss Nepal's first elected government headed by the same party.

The response of Prime Minister Manmohan Singh's government, too, echoed Jawaharlal Nehru's in response to the ouster of B.P. Koirala's government. The king had assaulted freedom and India, as the world's most populous democracy, had the moral obligation to do something. In December 1960, India could not do much because of China. Maybe Beijing could be the unofficial excuse for New Delhi to do more.

The story was far more complicated. India had declared the Nepalese Maoists as terrorists well before Nepal had done so. Yet senior Maoist leaders enjoyed safe haven on Indian soil. Chronic squabbling by Nepal's notoriously fractious political parties and an inexplicable royal palace massacre fuelled their 'people's war'. India armed the Nepalese military to fight the rebels, whose leaders were safe on Indian soil to compose ever-convoluted statements against New Delhi. From China, successive Nepalese governments were under pressure to crush the rebellion. Counterintuitively, for half a century, China's communist rulers had considered the Nepalese monarchy an anchor of stability and guarantor of their interests.

Nepal was in a no-win situation. Just as the worsening relations between the two Asian giants had cast their shadow on the Himalayan state's internal politics in the early 1960s, improving Sino-Indian ties were tightening the pressure three decades later. Chinese arms import by the palace-led partyless regime of King Birendra had angered New Delhi in 1989. But Rajiv Gandhi and Deng Xiaoping had embarked on a new partnership the previous year. Thus, New Delhi, having failed to bring a recalcitrant Kathmandu to its knees through a trade and transit embargo, backed a burgeoning democracy movement. China, preoccupied with the aftermath of the Tiananmen Square massacre, saw the restoration of multiparty democracy in Nepal as Indian-inspired regime change. Still, Beijing publicly counselled Kathmandu to improve relations with New Delhi.

Pacified, India spent the rest of the 1990s depicting Nepal as a haven for Pakistan's Inter-Services Intelligence-backed subversives. It felt vindicated in December 1999 when an Indian Airlines flight to New Delhi was hijacked from Kathmandu to Kandahar via Punjab and Dubai. The hijackers, linked to Kashmiri separatists, not only freed key allies in Indian prisons but also forced upon Indian Foreign Minister Jaswant Singh the ignominy of having to escort them to Kandahar. A year later, rumours surfaced that the Bollywood heartthrob of the season had said somewhere that he did not like the Nepalese. No one seemed to know where Hrithik Roshan had made the remark. But it was enough to spark days of rioting in Kathmandu.

As the general political disorder continued to fuel the Maoist insurgency, the Chinese began boosting political and military contacts with King Birendra. The palace and the mainstream parties competed to play the Maoists off against each other. The wily rebels courted both, as the world's only Hindu kingdom's relationship with the Hindu nationalist-led government in India deteriorated. The constitutional monarch, reportedly in negotiations with the Maoist leadership, was contemplating intervention, possibly in consultation with the Chinese.

Instead, King Birendra and nine other members of the royal family, including Queen Aishwarya, were murdered inside a heavily fortified Narayanhity Palace, allegedly by a drink- and drug-crazed Crown Prince Dipendra, who then shot himself.

Having been crowned for two days under a coma, Dipendra, too, died, supposedly of self-inflicted gunshot wounds during the carnage. Prince Gyanendra, the sole surviving heir, was crowned amid widespread public suspicions of his complicity in the carnage. A crafty businessman and palace hardliner, he could not have been absent from the family gathering just by chance, could he? The next storyline was ready, but it was not good enough for the Maoists, who were as stunned as any other Nepalese. Ever ready to extract political mileage, they broadened the narrative to blame the new king and the incumbent prime minister for the massacre under a US-backed Indian plan to 'Sikkimise/Bhutanise' Nepal.

Having placed all its eggs in the palace basket, China woke up to the June 2001 palace massacre devastated enough. Nepal's notoriously creative rumour mill even ventured a reason or two why Beijing might have wanted to do away with the monarchy. With China's record of unconditional support for Nepal's royalty, ideological incompatibility was not considered credible enough a motive. Even the silliest conspiracy theorist was sensible enough to recognise this was a province of sleuths and snipers. CIA, RAW, but the Chinese? Did they even have a spy agency anyone knew about?

This was no laughing matter for Beijing. Three months later, the post-9/11 global war on terrorism had brought American arms and ammunition to China's doorstep. All to combat Nepalese Maoists whom Beijing had disowned only because it saw them as misguided adherents of the Great Helmsman. In the geostrategic whirlwind, the rest of the world would have no time for these fine distinctions or Nepal's wider convolutions.

New Delhi, like Washington and Beijing, had acquiesced in – and perhaps even instigated – King Gyanendra's takeover of full executive powers in October 2002. Frustrated by New Delhi's apathy in ending the refuge Nepalese Maoists continued enjoying on Indian soil, the monarch contemplated bolder action. Around this time, the Maoists had sent feelers to the Bharatiya Janata Party-led government of Prime Minister Atal Behari Vajpayee, while escalating their rhetorical war on India. Palace intelligence sources discovered that Nepalese Maoists were being trained in the shadowy elite Establishment-22 camp in Chakrata, Uttarakhand a month before Nepal's anti-rebel Armed Police Force arrived for their drills. (Shah, 2010). Both developments would not become public until years later.

Caught between competing American and Chinese assertiveness in an area it traditionally considered its turf, India was opposed to further independent royal action. India's growing alliance with the United States only added to Beijing's apprehensions. If the palace felt confident enough to strike, New Delhi surmised the Chinese must have had something to do with it.

Something for sure, but not all that much, it turned out. Although Chinese Premier Wen Jiabao skipped Nepal during his South Asia tour, Foreign Minister Li Zhaoxing arrived in Kathmandu as part of 50th-anniversary celebrations of diplomatic relations. Li met with King Gyanendra and handed an invitation from Chinese President Hu Jintao to the king to the flagship annual Boao regional economic forum. There had been widespread speculation that China would step into the breach after India and Britain suspended sales of weapons to Nepal. However, in a pre-departure news conference, Li said he had not discussed security matters with Nepalese officials.

Clearly, the Chinese were not too keen to ruffle Indian feathers amid an upswing in bilateral ties.

Nor was China about to abandon Nepal. The kingdom had stood by Beijing during its early decades of international isolation after the establishment of the People's Republic in 1949. Foreign Minister Li's arrival in Kathmandu may not have been the full-throated support the royal regime expected, but it was too much for New Delhi's liking.

India was unsure of what to do next. Divisions persisted among key institutions on how to address the royal takeover. The Indian military, with close traditional ties with its Nepalese counterpart, and the Home Ministry, fighting a raging Maoist rebellion within, were looking for ways of engaging with the palace. The External Affairs Ministry and the intelligence agencies wanted to pursue a more radical approach, one that would chasten the pesky palace and reverse Nepal's geostrategic drift away from India's orbit.

The royal regime's crackdown on political leaders and activists under a state of emergency forestalled any significant protests for several weeks. When the opposition recovered from the initial blow, protests were scattered and still limited to party cadres, members of fraternal organisations and allies in civil society. New Delhi's sustained pressure on King Gyanendra to cede power to the mainstream parties had failed to make much headway amid the apathy of ordinary Nepalese. The people had had enough of the constant squabbling, shady deals and crude contest for power that followed the restoration of multiparty democracy in 1990.

Opposition politicians who evaded the royal dragnet arrived in New Delhi and set up camp there. King Gyanendra dispatched emissaries to New Delhi to explain his compulsions and to elicit support in traditional constituencies. The Maoist rebels, caught in the most severe internal conflict in their decade-long insurgency, struggled to determine whether they should consider India or the monarchy their principal adversary.

Officially, the Indian government reiterated the urgency of reconciliation between the monarch and the mainstream parties. The United States and Britain began consulting with India on a coordinated response. China, albeit quietly, calibrated its engagement with the palace within the framework of its own improving relations with India. Indian politicians, notably of the Marxist variant, proposed and worked on building a Maoist-mainstream alliance against the royal regime.

Bad To Worse

Nepal's situation turned from bad to worse in the ensuing months. Although the public still tolerated the royal takeover from the bickering politicians, the king had few allies. He turned to the gerontocratic remnants of the partyless Panchayat system era. Fettered by the past, age had enfeebled them. The younger ministers were too notorious or political novices. The unity in the mainstream opposition parties prevented significant defections. The Maoists were growing more aggressive amid growing international criticism of the monarchy.

When King Gyanendra requested a meeting with Premier Manmohan Singh on the sidelines of the Bandung Conference, Indian diplomats did not want to hear any of it. Through back channels, a meeting was arranged. In interactions with reporters, the monarch had an upbeat assessment of what he had agreed with New Delhi. In fact, too upbeat for India's liking.

The palace-friendly elements who arranged the meeting were incensed by the royal entourage's eagerness to put a positive spin on things that might have casually come up during the talks. Relations chilled during the subsequent weeks as New Delhi detected clear signs of a palace intent on entrenching itself in power.

In New Delhi, reports started appearing of how Indian intelligence agents were 'chaperoning' Maoist leader Pushpa Kamal Dahal 'Prachanda' and the party's chief ideologue Baburam Bhattarai around the corridors of power. Mainstream Nepalese opposition leaders, who had formally banded into a Seven Party Alliance (SPA), began flying into New Delhi at the same time, often on the same flight. Shyam Saran, the former ambassador in Kathmandu, had been promoted to Foreign Secretary. During engagements with China as part of the two countries' strategic dialogue, he appeared to have persuaded Beijing to dilute its support to the Nepalese monarchy. India would make sure China did not lose much. In February 2006, a year into the royal takeover, a Chinese Foreign Ministry spokesperson made an unprecedented statement warning King Gyanendra to seek compromise (Dixit, 2010). The United States, anxious to secure Indian ratification of the bilateral civil nuclear deal, had to contend with the Indian Marxists supporting the Indian government. The Europeans, assured of their security under the American umbrella, could afford to become more creative about identity, gender and inclusion as the route to newness.

It was against this backdrop that the SPA and the Communist Party of Nepal (CPN)-Maoist signed a 12-point understanding in New Delhi, specifying that 'autocratic monarchy' was the main problem in Nepal and that both sides (the parties and the Maoists) had made mistakes. The agreement also outlined that the way forward was (1) to topple 'autocratic monarchy', (2) for the Maoists to participate in multiparty politics, and (3) for there to be elections to a constituent assembly, which would draw up a new Constitution. The Maoists gave a "firm commitment to acceptance of [a] competitive multiparty system, [the] fundamental rights of the people, human rights, and the rule of law and democratic principles and values and to act accordingly."

Indian officialdom kept a low profile on the extent of its involvement in securing the deal, mindful of traditional Nepalese suspicions of New Delhi's motives and intentions. Sections of the Indian media were less reticent. Perhaps New Delhi was impelled by a desire to continue the engagement with the royal government. The summit of the South Asian Association for Regional Cooperation in Dhaka – cancelled the previous year ostensibly because India refused to legitimise the monarch – proved to be a turning point. India contemplated a last-ditch effort to persuade King Gyanendra to restore democracy. The ruler had other ideas. He proposed that China be inducted as an observer to the regional organisation at the same time it welcomed Afghanistan as a full member. New Delhi saw that as a brazen attempt by Nepal to flash the 'China card'. But it turned out the monarch also spoke for Bangladesh, Pakistan and Sri Lanka. Under the complex rules governing South Asian collective self-reliance, New Delhi was forced to give Beijing a seat so close to the table.

Regardless of what really happened in Dhaka – as the published conflicting recollections of key players in both countries would later force us to wonder – the instant storyline was too good to discard. As some Indian editorial writers openly called for punishing the palace, New Delhi stepped up ways of implementing the 12-point understanding. Already disenchanted by the palace's repeated promises of restoring democracy, the Americans went along with the Indians, still making perfunctory noises about the Maoists' motives and intentions. The delivery of truckloads of Chinese arms to Nepal weeks later hardened New Delhi's stand against the palace. The history of India's involvement in Nepalese affairs prompted many to question whether New Delhi was actively pushing all three sides into an intractable conflict to further its own ends.

If the Chinese were cognisant of that history, they were also growing upset by the royal regime's characterisation that it enjoyed Beijing's unconditional support. State Councillor Tang Jiaxuan postponed what was to have marked the arrival of the highest-ranking Chinese dignitary since the royal takeover. When he did land in Kathmandu a few weeks later, Tang sprung a surprise by engaging with opposition leaders as well as the palace. By February 2006, a year into the royal takeover, Beijing had become exasperated by the palace's inability to reach out to a broader spectrum of society to stabilise the country. But it still feared an imposed recipe for democracy would open the door wider to intervention and coercion by India and western governments, especially the United States. That was one of the fundamental reasons for China's opposition to the US-led agenda aimed at forcing King Gyanendra to give up direct rule, one Chinese analyst said. (Zhang, 2006) Unsentimental pragmatism, that enduring characteristic of Chinese foreign policy, surfaced quite openly. Tang had arrived to convey the first message from Beijing to reserve its diplomatic backing for certain political forces other than the monarchy, according to the same Chinese analyst.

As the democracy protests grew in stridency in early April 2006, the government became harsher in its crackdown, intensifying the unrest. Tens of thousands of protesters defied curfews every day to challenge royal authority. As the United States, Britain, China, and the European Union pressed for a compromise, Prime Minister Singh sent a special envoy to the palace. For many Nepalese, India's intervention was too tentative – and even intriguing. Prime Minister Singh entrusted Karan Singh, a Congress veteran who had served as foreign minister, with nudging King Gyanendra towards compromise. But most Nepalese knew Karan Singh not only as the last regent of Jammu and Kashmir but also as someone related through marriage to the Nepalese royal household. Now New Delhi's motives came under suspicion from the mainstream parties and the Maoist rebels.

The monarch's call to the SPA to form a new government, ostensibly Karan Singh's formula, drew instant applause from New Delhi. But it failed to calm the streets of Kathmandu. Amid angry protests in Kathmandu, New Delhi was forced to revise its position by conspicuously omitting references to the monarchy. King Gyanendra, through a second proclamation, restored the House of Representatives and handed over power to the SPA and allowed them to choose a prime minister. The constitutionality or otherwise of the move was irrelevant. It represented the triumph of the Nepalese people. India, by then, had alienated all three Nepalese players.

In retrospect, Beijing's intentions were visible early on.

Having supported the Royal Nepal Army's operations against the Maoist rebels towards the very end, Beijing conveniently replaced its ambassador in Kathmandu the following year. The new Chinese envoy became the first foreign representative to present credentials to the prime minister concurrently acting as head of state. The substance of this move would eventually outweigh its symbolism.

Beijing began boosting contacts with the Maoists and asserting that unlike India and the United States, it had not considered the rebels terrorists. China just objected to the Nepalese rebels' misappropriation of the Great Helmsman name and use of tactics specific to Chinese conditions of a bygone era. In other words, the terrorist tag desecrated Mao's memory. With such sweet reasonableness and the political heft that Beijing could bring, Nepalese Maoists could focus squarely on the future.

China was only one of many foreign actors India confronted in Nepal. The United States and the European Union – including member countries in their individual capacity – had a plethora of ideas, as did an assortment of international non-governmental organisations. In a set of moves and manoeuvres replete with the intricacies of Kabuki, as the following chapters shall narrate, Nepal embarked on newness that was no less nebulous. One compromise perfunctorily redefined another no less peremptorily. The international community legitimised everything in the name of hope and change. A decade later, not a few Nepalese still animated by the slogans resonating throughout the uprising of April 2006 were left wondering where the Constitution's three pillars of republicanism, secularism and federalism had come from. Prime Minister

Girija Koirala, when he was still battling the Maoists with the full force of the state, had rejected their idea of a constituent assembly, saying it would open a Pandora's box. The mere prospect of one now had raised the lid all the way up.

Provisional Posturing

AS THE REINSTATED House of Representatives met on April 28, 2006 for its first session, the visitors' gallery was bustling with the chiefs of the diplomatic missions and top United Nations representatives. Communist Party of India-Marxist (CPM) leader Sitaram Yechury led an Indian delegation into the chamber to express solidarity with the Nepalese people in their moment of triumph. One person was conspicuous by his absence: Indian ambassador Shiv Shankar Mukherjee. The Indian Embassy explained that the ambassador, not having received the invitation in time, had scheduled another engagement outside Kathmandu. Others attributed his absence to New Delhi's desire to display a hands-off approach as Nepal embarked on an alternative course. One legislator went on the record in the chamber to describe Mukherjee's absence as 'significant'.

Three weeks later, a more festive atmosphere descended on Nepal as the House of Representatives convened to adopt what was being called the local variant of the Magna Carta. Besides removing the word 'Hindu' from the official description of the country, the parliament the monarch had just resurrected declared itself sovereign and the king subject to it. The term 'royal' was removed from all important state institutions to underscore the country's apparent break from its past. That included the Royal Nepal Army, which was thought to have played a leading role in persuading the king to cede power after having received assurances of continued support from India.

The May 18 proclamation ran into controversy as it emerged that transforming Nepal from a Hindu state into a secular one was not part of the plan. People close to Prime Minister Girija Prasad Koirala insist to this day that the text abolishing Nepal's Hindu statehood was not in the draft the cabinet had endorsed and forwarded to parliament for adoption. It did appear in the text Speaker Subhas Nembang read out to members on an ailing Koirala's behalf before they overwhelmingly endorsed it. Some insist that someone had inserted 'secular' in pencil at the last moment.

The proclamation was the subject of much disagreement before the cabinet endorsed the final text. There was concern whether Nepal could sustain the radical break the Maoists sought. Despite their antipathy for King Gyanendra, key elements in the CPN-Unified Marxist-Leninist (UML) and the Nepali Congress were uneasy about stripping from the monarch the supreme commandership of the army. The politically ascendant Maoists, after all, were still armed. Secularism, too, was a divisive issue in a country with an overwhelmingly Hindu population. Days earlier, Koirala had assured representatives of indigenous nationalities that Nepal would become a secular state. If Koirala had relented in the cabinet's text, he must have done so in deference to the counterargument. Had the Maoists put last-minute pressure on the mainstream parties? Were foreign groups uncomfortable with Nepal's existence as the world's only officially Hindu state prepared to strike at religion harder than at the royals? Swept under the headiness of the moment as they were, such questions would continue to haunt Nepal.

Two weeks earlier, King Gyanendra had sworn Koirala into office. In a break from tradition, all other ministers took their oaths from the prime minister. As the first politician who demanded the restoration of parliament hours after the king dissolved in 2002 at the recommendation of an elected prime minister, Koirala evoked ridicule from many in the opposition. Even as they stepped up protests against the palace's growing peremptoriness, Koirala's allies did not see reinstatement as a viable road back to democracy. Yet he persisted and felt vindicated. Now he moved swiftly to assuage the Maoists, who were worried about their exclusion from power, by announcing an immediate vote in favour of the principle of a constituent assembly, a longstanding rebel demand. The Maoists withdrew their threat to blockade district headquarters and announced a formal three-month ceasefire. The rebels gradually emerged 'above ground' to claim a respectable place in the interim government. The monarch, barred from receiving ambassadors and a plethora of state duties, was now to be questioned about his conduct as chair of the deposed council of ministers. Predictably, the king refused to answer to the high-level panel the government had set up to investigate atrocities against the 19-day popular protests.

Although discordant notes sounded here and there, the normalisation process had made an agreeable start. Since issues of constitutionalism would remain in the backseat for a while, political imperatives were expected to drive the tenure, remit and jurisdiction of the revived House of Representatives. By annulling the municipal elections the royal regime had organised, compensating families of 'martyrs' and setting up the judicial commission to probe the royal regime's excesses, the government had created the necessary conditions to focus on the big picture.

For all their bluster, the Maoists, too, seemed ready to engage with the Koirala government. Despite the mainstream parties and the Maoists incessantly warning the people to beware 'royal conspiracies', the palace was going to remain a player – at least, for now. Koirala intended to proceed towards the CA polls after drawing the Maoists into an interim government. That way, he could ensure the rebels' commitment to the integrity of the process and the sanctity of the outcome. The tasks of reaching out to the insurgents and drawing up the modalities for a new elected assembly could proceed on parallel tracks.

Discontent within the SPA over the allotment of ministerial portfolios and the speakership of the reinstated lower house could not be dismissed outright as a reversion to the parties' inherent weakness for power. Civil society felt entitled to admonishing the political leadership every step of the way, given their poor record in the 1990s. Without their supervision, the street protests could not have gained the legitimacy and impact they did.

With its principal aim achieved, the SPA required a different adhesive to remain relevant. Without proper distribution of responsibility, the constituents could not be expected to unite behind a shared endeavour. A more judicious distribution of ministerial portfolios was essential to maintain the political balance needed to sustain the open and transparent system envisaged. With the Maoists on board, the challenge of reconciling ideological and procedural disagreements would become more daunting.

Given the politically charged atmosphere, the CA elections had been primarily linked to the future of the monarchy. In days and weeks ahead, the SPA and the Maoists would recognise the perils inherent in such a narrow frame of reference. During the drafting phase of the 1990 Constitution, such issues as exclusion, oppression, distributive injustice had been dismissed as distractions from democracy's consolidation. The country paid a heavy price for such haughtiness. Now those issues held the key to Nepal's collective salvation.

More troubling, however, were the critical questions relating to the external dynamics of Nepal's conflict. US Assistant Secretary of State Richard Boucher, explaining why he did not meet with the king during his visit to Kathmandu, emphasised that the palace had ceased to be a political player. At the same time, Boucher defended his meeting with Army Chief Gen. Pyar Jung Thapa, saying the United States continued to view the military as an essential player. How much of Boucher's stance on the monarchy stemmed from the political atmosphere prevailing on the streets? What kind of role did the United States envisage for the Nepal Army?

Boucher's elevation of the military could not be divorced from domestic efforts to re-brand the institution. What kind of resistance would the military mount to any reorganisation effort? When the time came for creating a national army, could the United States, so bitterly opposed to the Maoist political leadership, accept the integration of ideologically driven former guerrillas? Persistent reports in the Indian media suggested that New Delhi, too, desired to build on its traditional relations with the Nepal Army. How 'national' could the military be with Washington and New Delhi vying for influence?

Despite its principal role in defusing the immediate crisis, India had emerged bruised. If there was any consensus among Indians about their latest experience in Nepal, it was that they had alienated the palace, parties and Maoists. India would undoubtedly prefer a modicum of stability in Nepal in the run-up to the CA elections to craft a more coherent policy. Would the political and institutional schisms already evident in New Delhi permit one?

The Indian Army and the internal security apparatus would watch the Maoists' transformation as part of their overall threat perception. New Delhi could share Washington's dilemma vis-à-vis the creation of a national army in Nepal. China, the most silent stakeholder in Nepalese stability, was unlikely to lose its faith in quiet diplomacy. Had the royal regime, behind the heat and dust of the democracy movement, reached any security-related accords with Beijing? If so, how far could the new government go toward revising or even annulling them without discomfiture in public? That underscored the crux of the crisis. For all the noise about autocracy, King Gyanendra's takeover was also driven by the urgency of consolidating Nepal's space between the two Asian giants. Regardless of the fate of the monarchy, Nepal's geostrategic vulnerabilities would persist.

Indian Quandary

For now, a legislature brought back from the dead was showing remarkable political life. Its members, too, were exhibiting uncharacteristic civility. The SPA and the Maoists had largely desisted from exulting in an air of finality. Deep inside, each was not entirely confident of the other's motive. Publicly, though, each remained confident of moulding the other in its spirit, if not in shape. Since political expediency would continue taking precedence over constitutionalism in the near term, the 'Magna Carta' would remain the locus. The apparent open-ended tenure of the resurrected legislature had rankled the rebels, but engagement with the SPA remained their best route to reshaping the state.

India had reinforced its status as the principal external stakeholder. The mainstream parties and the Maoists saw New Delhi as a guarantor of the peace agreement. For the Maoists, who were still wearing the terrorist tag in many essential world capitals, India was their preeminent source of international recognition and legitimacy. With New Delhi on their side, the mainstream parties felt more comfortable to thwart potential mischief from the royalist right as well as the Maoists.

What was becoming disturbing, though, was India's quandary. The anti-government sections of the political class and the media had been savaging Prime Minister Singh for virtually subcontracting Nepal policy to his CPM allies. The establishment of a secular Nepal had begun to worry constituencies beyond the Hindu nationalist Bharatiya Janata Party (BJP). For many Indians, it seemed the world's only Hindu republic would still have had contemporary relevance. More vocal sections of the BJP began seeing the developments in Nepal as less a permanent defeat for the world's only Hindu monarchy than a temporary triumph for the Indian left. Throughout King Gyanendra's direct rule, the BJP was reluctant to openly support the monarchy given the breakdown in India's relations with Nepal. The BJP's concern over the secularisation of the Nepalese state now allowed the party to back the retention of a constitutional monarchy.

All this underscored the reality that the turn of events in Nepal owed much to the peculiarities of India's domestic politics. The Indian left could not have led the initiative to forge the SPA-Maoist accord had it not held the key to the survival of the Singh coalition. But, then, were CPM leader Yechury's overt initiatives genuinely aimed at bolstering the democratic mainstream in Nepal against an assertive palace? Or was he merely the public face of the Indian left's effort to pre-empt a challenge from Indian Naxalites by subverting their ties with the Nepalese Maoists?

The looming prospect of a reinstated legislature gaining an eternal life must have riled the Maoists, especially amid public expectations of a brief session paving the way for an interim government and CA elections. Almost identical assertions from Washington and New Delhi making the Maoists' participation in an interim government contingent on their disarming must have been the tipping point. The CPM's advice to Indian Naxalites to follow their Nepalese allies' example of moderation could have only added insult to the Maoists' festering injuries.

The promptness with which Indian editorial writers and analysts linked the Maoists' harassment of Indians in Nepal to the rebels' reported contacts with Chinese emissaries provided the broader setting for analysis. Throughout the decade-long insurgency in Nepal, India benefited from the global perception that Beijing was behind the conflict. The ideology and the suffix the rebels carried obscured the ease with which the Nepalese Maoists enjoyed safe haven – if not overt official support – across the southern border.

New Delhi had grown increasingly sceptical of China's motives in South Asia, especially since Beijing received observer status in the South Asian Association for Regional Cooperation. The slightest sign of a Chinese-Maoist connection was bound to raise passions in India. To assuage New Delhi's concerns, Koirala led a 43-member delegation on a goodwill visit to India in early June. Prime Minister Singh, in a rare gesture, received him at Indira Gandhi International Airport and he would describe Koirala as South Asia's senior statesman. During official talks, the two leaders agreed that the restoration of democracy in Nepal provided a historic opportunity for qualitative enhancement of bilateral relations. Kathmandu and New Delhi reaffirmed their commitment to "impart a new dimension and dynamism in their relations based on the principles of peaceful coexistence, sovereign equality, territorial integrity, mutual respect and understanding."

Singh welcomed Koirala's initiative to consolidate the achievements of the popular movement by finding a peaceful solution to the armed conflict, restoring political stability and moving towards economic reconstruction for the welfare of the people. Stressing that India wished to see a strong, democratic, secular and prosperous neighbour, Singh said it was up to the Nepalese to decide the fate of King Gyanendra. In an initiative quickly dubbed a 'Himalayan Marshall Plan', New Delhi announced a Rs.10 billion reconstruction and development aid package in the form of immediate budgetary support, lines of credit, waiver of dues and investments.

While Koirala was busy in consultations in the Indian capital, Maoist leader Prachanda warned that his visit could be part of a 'deep conspiracy' by foreign powers to destroy the pact between his party and the SPA. "When there should be a political settlement first in Nepal, Koirala goes to India to bring money, an (assistance) package and hydropower pacts," he said. Prachanda expressed concern at the 'greater propaganda' coming from New Delhi about its upcoming economic package. This, he said, could be an effort to delude the Nepalese into believing that India could resolve Nepal's problems (Upadhya, 2008).

During his visit, Koirala could persuade New Delhi to accept a role for the United Nations as a way of checking the Maoists (Jha, 2012). One Indian newspaper editorial, underscoring a significant shift, urged New Delhi to shed its opposition to international mediation in Nepal's peace process and dispel Kathmandu's notion that India was playing the neighbourhood bully. Another advised India to offer economic aid, advice, and other assistance to help democracy strike roots in the country, arguing that an unstable Nepal had negative implications for India. Still another insisted that New Delhi work assiduously with all constituencies in Nepal to project the fact that India was best placed in the region to facilitate the transition to a functional and secure democracy (Upadhya, 2008).

The June 16 eight-point accord between the SPA and the Maoists and Prachanda's emergence in public may have stabilised the process. Still, the discord within SPA over specific provisions of the deal, and differences within Koirala's Nepali Congress on the prime minister's support of a ceremonial monarchy, were illustrative of the challenges the peace process confronted. As Dahal – as Prachanda would now prefer to be known – and Bhattarai returned to Kathmandu after touring their base areas to sell the accord to the rank and file, the Maoists' credibility as a peace partner came into sharper focus. Over the years, Dahal's perceived eloquence in expounding ideology had been useful in perpetuating the ambiguity the rebels used to build and wreck alliance among and within rival power centres. His public emergence had shifted the debate to whether he could tolerate enough internal dissent the multiparty system presupposed. More broadly, was peace the real agenda of the entire rebel organisation?

Plagued by similar questions, Beijing sent fact-finding missions on multiple fronts. In April, a Chinese team rushed to Nepal to extend an olive branch to the new government. Beijing's concerns were familiar, but it began expressing them with uncharacteristic candour. A key one related to Washington's process of resettling Tibetan refugees in Nepal. Deputy Prime Minister Khadga Prasad Sharma Oli told parliament that Chinese Foreign Minister Li Zhaoxing had raised the matter with him during a meeting in Geneva. Oli said Beijing had virtually accused Kathmandu of issuing refugee identification cards to "illegal migrants," taking it as a serious bilateral issue. As Beijing planned to send a representative to Kathmandu to lodge an official complaint, Chinese troops opened fire on a group of 70 Tibetans trying to cross into Nepal, killing at least two.

In July, Vice Foreign Minister Wu Tawei arrived on a three-day visit to offer increased assistance and seek reassurance that Nepal's new government continued its 'one China' policy. The same month, three Chinese government officials reportedly made a secret trip for talks with top Maoist leaders. Ai Ping, director-general of the International Department of the Communist Party of China, headed a delegation in August to discuss ways of enhancing bilateral economic, social and cultural issues.

Many Nepalese appeared reassured of the Maoists' sincerity by their remarkable restraint at a massive rally in Kathmandu. Still, top military strategist Ram Bahadur Thapa 'Badal' had gone silent, while his fellow Maoist commander Nanda Kishor Pun 'Pasang' was voicing scepticism. Portending things to come, the most prominent Maoist leader from the Terai, Matrika Yadav, threatened to boycott the CA elections unless Madhesis (Nepalese of Indian ethnicity living in the southern plains) got citizenship certificates.

Although parliament had voted swiftly to increase the political and administrative representation of women, similar measures for other traditionally marginalised groups such as janajatis (indigenous peoples), dalits (ex-'untouchables') and Madhesis were deferred. Critical questions persisted on the stockpiles of Maoist arms and ammunition, and the confinement of the national and rebel armies to barracks. The election's fairness would depend on how effectively others could stop Maoist intimidation.

A plan to invite the United Nations to oversee a system of 'double locks' – whereby arms would be kept under lock by both armies themselves and also by the UN – ran aground on differences concerning the form such an invitation should take. As delays on the matter raised fears for the peace process, general lawlessness began creeping into the rural Terai areas along the vast, porous and largely unregulated border with

India. A breakaway Maoist group claimed responsibility for the assassination of a member of parliament and former minister and issued threats to people at hills living in the region. Many local militias sprung up in response to the Maoists' unabated extortions.

As the first anniversary of the 12-point understanding approached, it became more apparent that India stood on flimsier ground than it did on the 1951 Delhi Compromise. It was telling that Maoist chief ideologue Dr Baburam Bhattarai could praise India for facilitating the accord and in the same breath blame New Delhi for conspiring to keep the rebels out of power. India must have been no less baffled by how the Maoists, who vowed to launch massive peaceful urban protests in case the talks failed, could still keep their broader pledge to turn South Asia into "a flaming field of Maoist revolutions".

Such fiery rhetoric could not obscure the Maoists' flexibility, though. An organisation that rose against the monarchy and parliamentary parties had now climbed down to ally with the latter. The Maoists had now distilled their original 40-point list of grievances heavily targeted at India into a diatribe against the monarchy. And that, too, through India's active facilitation.

Given the enormity of the undertaking, it was perhaps essential for the SPA and the Maoists to leave certain ambiguities in their accord. However, it would be naïve to think Dahal and Bhattarai signed on without having received private assurances on critical issues. Dahal had acknowledged that Indian officialdom had played a significant role in creating the broad anti-palace alliance. It would be safe to assume that the Maoists considered New Delhi the principal guarantor of its interpretation of the unfolding political course in Nepal.

In November, the SPA and the Maoists signed a Comprehensive Peace Accord (CPA). They would form an interim legislature from existing members of parliament, barring those who had opposed the people's movement. The Maoists would get seats along with unrepresented parties, professional organisations, and representatives of backward regions. The two sides agreed to hold elections in June 2007 to a 425-member constituent assembly, with 205 members chosen by the 'first-past-the-post' system, 204 by proportional representation, and 16 nominated by the government. The constituent assembly would decide on the future of the monarchy. The CPN-UML, which considered a referendum a better way of determining the issue, entered a note of dissent.

According to the agreement, Maoist fighters were to be confined to camps with their arms under lock and key monitored by the United Nations. The Nepalese government would feed them. The Nepal Army was also to be restricted to its barracks. A tripartite agreement among the UN, the government, and the Maoists on arms management followed the CPA. Ever since it became a member of the organisation in 1955, Nepal had remained comfortable with the presence of the United Nations.

It had taken the country six years to join the organisation, after the Soviet Union foiled its first effort in May 1949. Moscow believed Nepal's 1923 Treaty with British India had compromised its independence and sovereignty, thereby making the country ineligible for UN membership. It did not matter that the Soviet republics of Ukraine and Byelorussia were full members, giving Moscow three seats in the world body until 1991. Nepal then found itself frozen out during the early Cold War chill that had stalled UN membership expansion altogether. Nepal was finally admitted in 1955 after the Soviet Union agreed to a package deal allowing 16 new members into the world body. Considering the UN as a safeguard of its independence, Nepal had played an active role in peacekeeping missions around the world.

When Nepalese parties sought UN monitoring in the peace process, suspicions of India also guided them. New Delhi and Beijing had reservations because of their respective problems in Kashmir and Tibet. Yet suspicions of each other and their common distrust of others drew them closer to a limited UN mission.

Later in November, Maoist leader Dahal made his first public visit to India. The primary purpose was to take part in a global leadership conference attended by, among others, Prime Minister Singh and Congress President Sonia Gandhi. The Indian government publicly distanced itself from Dahal's visit, and no senior government official or Congress leader met the Maoist leader.

Beyond the conference, the Delhi visit offered Dahal an opportunity to mount a public relations blitz. Accompanied by his deputy, Dr Baburam Bhattarai, Dahal met former premiers Vishwanath Pratap Singh and Inder Kumar Gujral as well as other Indian leaders. In a newspaper interview, Dahal revealed that Pakistan's Inter-Services Intelligence had once offered to help the Maoists, but that he had refused. A recurrent theme of his public comments in New Delhi, on the eve of President Hu Jintao's visit, was that the Maoists would never allow Nepal to become a part of a Western plot to pit the Asian giants against each other.

For some, Dahal's overtures – even obsequiousness – confirmed suspicions that at least some part of India's political and security establishment was behind the Maoist insurgency all along. Others saw the Maoist chair, like generations of Nepalese politicians before him, openly lobby for that indispensable Indian support. Following the royal regime's collapse, Dahal and his deputies had begun praising India's role in facilitating the SPA-Maoist alliance. The Maoist supremo's comments in New Delhi went the farthest in underscoring his U-turn vis-à-vis India. There was another intriguing element to the affair. Dahal had initially ruled out participation in the New Delhi conference. The Maoists' first formal meeting with Indian ambassador Shiv Mukherjee appeared to change Dahal's plan. (Upadhya, 2008)

In early 2007, the reinstated parliament promulgated an interim Constitution before dissolving itself, paving the way for a 330-member interim 'legislature-parliament'. The Nepali Congress, CPN-UML and Maoists almost equally shared 75 percent of the seats. The rest comprised all members of the old parliament except supporters of royal rule, and party nominees. The seemingly redundant term 'legislature-parliament' was a compromise between the Nepali Congress's wish to retain parliament and the Maoists' insistence on breaking from the 1990 Constitution.

Divided Nations

On January 23, 2007, the United Nations Security Council created a political mission in Nepal to oversee the peace process. By a unanimously adopted resolution, the Council decided that the UN Political Mission in Nepal (UNMIN), headed by a Special Representative of the Secretary-General, would have a 12-month mandate which could be terminated or extended depending on a request from the government. The careful wording on the duration was intended to assuage China, which had wanted the six-month mandate UN missions customarily got. Secretary-General Ban Ki-moon sought the UN's presence beyond the June election so that the mission could complete its task effectively. The Council also noted the Secretary-General's expectation that the operation "will be a focused mission of limited duration", a concession to China as well as India.

The Nepali Congress shared India's opposition to a conventional peacekeeping operation in Nepal. While cognisant of the recognition and legitimacy, the UN would confer to them as a party to the peace process; the Maoists also opposed foreign forces. Then there was underlying Nepalese sense of national pride. How could a longstanding contributor to peacekeeping operations now suddenly become a recipient. Nepalese stakeholders were committed and qualified to manage the post-conflict phase, unlike the 'failed states' needing extensive international support. A nationally owned peace process could tolerate only a limited United Nations role (Suhrke, 2011).

While the Nepalese widely hailed UNMIN's creation, Maoist supremo Dahal expressed reservations at the UN's decision to station observers for a year, since the election to the constituent assembly would be over in six months. His misgivings gained significance as it concurred with China's argument during closed-door consultations at UN headquarters. Beijing, for its part, now seemed more interested in healthy interactions among major powers considering Nepal's geostrategic importance. While recognising UN involvement as more relevant in that light, China was eager to ensure that UNMIN's role was measured and proportionate enough to produce positive effects (Zhang, 2006).

UNMIN would manage arms and armed personnel from both the government and CPN-Maoist, in line with the CPA. It would also provide technical support for the planning, preparation and conduct of the election of a constituent assembly in a free and fair atmosphere, in consultation with the parties; a small team of electoral monitors to review all technical aspects of the electoral process; and report on the conduct of the election.

The UN Security Council noted that both sides had asked for UN help in implementing key aspects of the peace deal, and also recognised the strong desire of the Nepalese people for peace and the restoration of democracy. The 15-member body further highlighted the need to pay special attention to the needs of women, children and traditionally marginalised groups in the peace process. That quest would go on to convulse Nepal the most. For now, an advance team of 35 UN monitors was already working to begin registering and storing weapons of the former combatants.

With the formal onset of the peace process, however, the Maoists' support base began splintering along regional, ethnic, and caste-based lines. The Terai became the first flashpoint. Grievances always existed in the plains against the domination of hills' people. But the Madhesi people had traditionally worked within national parties or joined the Maoists to achieve their aims. Regional protests erupted in late 2006 demanding proportional representation and regional autonomy within a federal structure.

On December 26, clashes broke out in the western Terai town of Nepalgunj between Madhesis and immigrants from the hills. The Madhesi Janadhikar Forum (MJF), a newly formed broad grouping led by former Maoist Upendra Yadav that also included members of mainstream parties, spearheaded further protests. In Kathmandu, MJF leaders were arrested for publicly burning the interim Constitution. The organisation responded by calling a general strike. When one MJF activist was shot dead in an ensuing clash with Maoist cadres in Lahan in the eastern Terai, violent protests erupted across much of the region, leading to 20 deaths over two weeks. The MJF's protests prompted counter demonstrations by the Chure-Bhavar Ekta Samaj, representing immigrants from the hills who had settled in the northern Terai and demanded a separate state.

The most serious incident occurred in March 2007, when MJF supporters clashed with outnumbered Maoist cadres in the city of Gaur in Rautahat district, killing 27 Maoists. The MJF was committed to non-violent protest, but many other groups in the Terai were not. The Goit and Jwala Singh factions of the Janatantrik Terai Mukti Morcha (JTMM), each led by renegade Maoists, claimed to be fighting for the full independence of the Terai. These and other groups warned civil servants of hill origin to leave the region or risk death, resulting in some 900 officials abandoning their posts. A group calling itself the 'Terai Army' claimed responsibility for three explosions in Kathmandu in September that killed two people and injured over 20. A Maoist-Madhesi clash in Kapilvastu, near Lord Buddha's birthplace, took a Hindu-Muslim hue.

Around this time, the Nepal Federation of Indigenous Nationalities (NEFIN) – whose member associations claimed to represent 59 different ethnic groups – was organising widespread protests. They, too, wanted elections for the constituent assembly to guarantee full proportional representation to the various ethnic groups. The mode agreed to in 2006 specified that half of the CA members would be elected by proportional representation (as preferred by the Maoists) and the other half by the first-past-the-post system (as favoured by the Nepali Congress). The NEFIN also demanded an immediate guarantee of a federal system in Nepal but, unlike the MJF, opposed a single 'Madhes' unit in the Terai. The NEFIN supported the Tharus and other ethnic groups that rejected the 'Madhes' label and wanted autonomy of their own. The government offered to hold talks with all groups.

As the Koirala government struggled to reconcile these demands, King Gyanendra stepped into the debate on February 19. In a message to the nation on Democracy Day, the monarch defended his 2005 takeover as a compulsion created by political parties. He accepted moral responsibility for the failures and successes of his 15-month direct rule and stressed the need for inclusivity in Nepal. Predictably, the mainstream parties and the Maoists were infuriated. Although the king traditionally delivered a message each year to mark the anniversary of the end of Rana rule in 1951, the interim Constitution had left the monarchy in a state of suspension.

Moreover, SPA constituents were incensed by the monarch's reference to the mainstream political parties as catalysts for his October 4, 2002 dismissal of Nepal's last elected government. The Maoists, who long claimed to have brought ethnic and regional discrimination to the world's attention, were already accusing the royalists of stoking the flames in the Terai to undermine the former rebels there. After the king's message, they began demanding the immediate abolition of the monarchy.

The interim Constitution was amended in March 2007 by including commitments to federalism, an increase in constituencies for the Terai region, and proportional representation for different ethnic groups and women within the administration. Another amendment two months later provided for the 240 proportionally elected seats in the assembly to be divided thus: 31 percent for Madhesis, 11 percent for Dalits, 37.8 percent for the 'indigenous' ethnic groups represented by the NEFIN, 4 percent for backward regions, and 30.2 percent for other groups, with half of the seats in each category going to women. The NEFIN later yielded on full proportional representation in return for a guarantee that all its 59 ethnic groups would have at least one member in the constituent assembly. The MJF also dropped its insistence on full proportional representation, purportedly under Indian pressure. Dissident members within both groups continued to protest what they considered a betrayal. Average Nepalese already were doubtful of free elections. The chief election commissioner complained of the lack of laws and personnel. Prime Minister Koirala pledged to adhere to the schedule despite similar doubts from within the ruling alliance.

After weeks of bluster and bargaining, the SPA and the Maoists formed an interim government on April 1. Resigning from a position King Gyanendra had sworn him into 11 months earlier, Koirala was now re-appointed premier by the interim legislature. The 22-member cabinet, including five Maoist ministers, pledged to hold elections to the constituent assembly on June 20. Soon, the Maoists began growing restive as the Nepali Congress continued to dominate the government.

The Maoists, complaining of being sidelined in major decisions, were also appalled by the living conditions for their 30,000 fighters in holding camps. Also of significant concern was the lack of progress on integrating the PLA into the national army. The CPA identified the 'democratisation and restructuring' of the Nepal Army as a core element of the peace process. The Maoists insisted on a comprehensive reform of the institution, including the induction of large numbers of Maoist combatants into its ranks.

In the midst of such political wrangling, the Koirala government made a vivid display of its eagerness to engage with China. At a summit of the South Asian Association for Regional Cooperation in New Delhi in April, Nepal made a strong pitch to include China as a full member of the eight-nation organisation. Prime Minister Koirala stressed the importance of expanding the organisation by including China during an interaction of SAARC leaders with Indian President APJ Abdul Kalam. China, along with South Korea, Japan, the United States and the European Union were invited for the first time as observers to the summit. The rivalry between India and China marred the inauguration of the summit amid reports that Beijing sought to dilute New Delhi's hold in the region as a major economic power. The dispute between the two Asian powers was one of several that underlined the discord within the body. The summit was aimed at injecting new momentum into an underperforming regional bloc by boosting trade and cooperation. The feud between New Delhi and Beijing began over the establishment of a regional development fund, seen as a key initiative for SAARC and expected to receive automatic approval. But the proposal ran into trouble over whether observer nations like China should be allowed to contribute to the fund.

Though China's inclusion enjoyed support among sections of Indian academia keen on accelerating economic cooperation, New Delhi's strategic anxieties about Beijing's ultimate motives in the region had restrained its official posture. India was opposed to China's participation in the development fund, believing it was seeking to strengthen its position through its financial prowess. Indian apprehensions had intensified after Chinese Foreign Minister Li Zhaoxing travelled to the summit via Islamabad, where he spoke enthusiastically about using the summit to "develop relations with South Asian countries" (Upadhya, 2008).

New Delhi's ambivalence towards the peace process was now becoming more apparent, as it showed little interest in implementing the CPA's other provisions, such as the establishment of a Truth and Reconciliation Commission and a commission to investigate disappearances. India strongly opposed provisions that would revamp the political structure and potentially increase the Maoists' power over the state military. The Maoists' ideas of 'merging' the two armies on equal terms and instituting substantive security-sector reforms, including the 'democratisation' of the Nepal Army, barely drew New Delhi's attention. The way India saw it, the Nepal Army had helped to turn the country away from the monarchy (Saran, 2018). Now it was the ultimate bulwark against a potential Maoist military takeover. India sought to prevent any action that could undermine the morale and institutional coherence of the army (Adhikari, 2014). From the perspective of New Delhi and the Nepalese generals, only a few thousand Maoist fighters could join the national army.

The Maoists suspended cooperation with UN staff verifying no one inside the camps were under the age of 18 and that all had joined the PLA before the agreed cut-off date of May 25, 2006. The Maoists' failure to restore confiscated lands to their owners as promised, their continued extraction of 'public donations', and their attacks against the activities of their rivals angered the other political parties. The focus of anger was the Maoist Young Communist League (YCL) and trade unions.

The postponement of the CA elections scheduled for June further infuriated the Maoists. They saw the delay as a deliberate ploy by the SPA and others to ensure the Maoists' popularity declined furthered. Although the Maoists agreed to a new election date of November 22, they made their participation conditional on the abolition of the monarchy and the adoption of full proportional representation before the vote.

Many expected the Maoists to trail both the Nepali Congress and the CPN-UML in the elections. Some speculated the former rebels wanted to avoid the voting. However, they sought to seize the initiative by pressing for concessions such as the immediate abolition of the monarchy. The Maoists also believed that full proportional representation would prevent the Nepali Congress from profiting from the split on the left. The Maoists announced a protest programme to achieve the two preconditions and later pulled out of the government after the expiry of their deadline.

In the Nepali Congress, Koirala had spoken several times of a 'ceremonial monarchy' but eventually turned in favour of republicanism. A vocal section of the Nepali Congress wanted to retain the monarchy to combat the preponderance of the left. Koirala was also believed to have come under increasing Indian pressure to endorse republicanism formally. New Delhi and sections of the Kathmandu establishment sought King Gyanendra's abdication and exile. However, Paras, the heir apparent, was more controversial than his father. The next in line, Prince Hridayendra, was a toddler. Koirala appeared to favour the concept of a 'baby king' wherein the executive head would act as regent.

Although the precise reasons for King Gyanendra's opposition were never made clear, it seemed he sought the regency for himself or Hridayendra's mother, Princess Himani. Even if she could physically assume the regency, Queen Mother Ratna, the senior-most royal, was constrained by the prevailing public reputation of her late husband, King Mahendra. Moreover, the new rulers had widened the succession space by providing for daughters to ascend to the throne. With King Gyanendra's daughter and two granddaughters along with slain King Birendra's two granddaughters available, the field was wide open.

While King Gyanendra had remained silent on the acceleration of events in April 2006, including India's role, his confidants had begun speaking out. One insisted that the monarch felt betrayed. New Delhi had apparently told the monarch that he if he ceded power to the SPA, he would retain an influential role as a ceremonial king. After the king reinstated the parliament, according to the confidant, India distanced itself from the monarchy, saying it was for the people to decide. "Then everything started to go wrong … the agenda coming from the south (India) was to remove the king, weaken the army and weaken religion. The king felt he had been set up" (Upadhya, 2008). The king would later state in a television interview that there was documentary evidence of the parties' agreement to retain the monarchy. While the Maoists had shut the door on any form of monarchy, the Nepali Congress continued to oppose complete abolition before the CA elections.

NC leaders hardened their stance on retaining the first-past-the-post system for half the assembly seats, believing it stood to benefit that way from the reunification of Sher Bahadur Deuba's Nepali Congress (Democratic) with its parent organisation. After protracted negotiations, the parties agreed to enlarge the constituent assembly to 601 seats with 240 elected on the old first-past-the-post system, 335 by proportional representation, and 26 nominated by the prime minister.

It was resolved that the country should at once be declared a 'federal democratic republic'. Formal implementation of this declaration would be delayed until the first session of the constituent assembly. After the interim parliament approved the deal, the Maoists rejoined the government at the end of the year.

India, viewing elections the best way to 'lock' the Maoists into mainstream democratic politics, shared growing expectations that they would rank a distant third. India's National Security Adviser M. K. Narayanan even went on record before the polls to state his preference for the Nepali Congress.

Although the peace process seemed to be back on track in the new year, discontent over the compromise within Maoist ranks and some ethnic activist along with continued unrest in parts of the country cast a long shadow. There was renewed disruption in the Terai where the United Madhesi Democratic Front (UMDF) – comprising the MJF and two other parties – demanded regional autonomy and greater representation. Protests were also held in the eastern hills by the National Republican Front, which included organisations claiming to represent the Limbu, Rai, Tamang, and other ethnic groups. The Koirala government rejected the UMDF's demand for a single autonomous Terai region owing to opposition by most national parties. Several Terai groups also opposed the demand because of wariness of the mainly high-caste leadership of the Madhesi movement.

Madhesis enjoyed close cultural and family links with Bihar and Uttar Pradesh states, and accommodation of their demands in the new Constitution remained a major priority for New Delhi. India feared that unrest in the Terai could spill over across the border. New Delhi also saw Madhesi leaders as important allies who could be expected to uphold Indian interests in Nepal.

India played a central role in consolidating Madhesi parties. It even encouraged several Madhesi leaders to quit the older parliamentary parties and form the Tarai Madhes Loktantrik Party (TMLP) in 2007 as a counterweight to the MJF. Indian officials in Kathmandu also continued pressuring the government to accept key Madhesi demands, including one ensuring that political parties in the Terai did not have to include hill candidates in their lists. At one point, a vexed Koirala would publicly muse that India could resolve the Madhes issue in a minute if it chose to do so.

Maoist Magic

Belying fears of widespread Maoist attacks, the April 2008 election campaign was relatively calm. The Maoists suffered the most fatalities with at least 15 cadres killed in police firing or politically motivated attacks. However, the former rebels made it virtually impossible for pro-monarchy parties to campaign. Election day was relatively peaceful, with four fatalities and reports of fraudulent voting at some booths. Surprisingly, the former Maoist insurgents won 30 percent of the popular vote and about half of the first-past-the-post seats. The increase in the percentage of seats filled through the proportional representation system meant that the Maoists won only 220 out of 575 elected seats in the 601-member CA overall.

The other parties winning seats through both systems were the Nepali Congress (110), CPN-UML (103), MJF (52), Terai Madhes Loktantrik Party (20), Sadbhavana Party (9), Janamorcha Nepal Party (7), and the Nepal Workers and Peasants Party (4). Sixteen other parties received seats under the proportional representation list only, and two independents won first-past-the-post seats. The rules required the parties fielding candidates for more than a fifth of the proportional representation seats to include specific percentages of the major ethnic groups in their lists. Prime Minister Koirala – who did not contest the election – saw his Nepali Congress lose support in the Terai to the MJF. He maintained his traditional grip on the party, while CPN-UML general secretary Madhav Kumar Nepal resigned from his post, accepting responsibility for the party's poor showing.

The Maoists seemed to have seen a surge in support towards the end of the campaign. They retained a core of committed cadres and supporters and campaigned more effectively than the other parties. They were careful to ensure ethnic balance in choosing candidates for first-past-the-post seats. The Maoists also benefited from public perceptions that they might return to violence if they failed to get electoral support. Another factor was the Maoists' intimidation of opposition candidates.

Before opponents could cry foul, international observers, including former US president Jimmy Carter, certified the elections as free and fair. The former rebels were poised to take democratically the power their guns had denied them. The Maoists' real motives remained a source of major concern within the country and outside. India, China, the United States and the European Union had varying degrees of apprehensions in different areas.

China's focus was on developments that took place in parallel with the election campaign. Between March and August 2008, Tibetan refugees living in the country mounted their most organised protests in the past 50 years. The previous October, the US Congress conferred the Congressional Gold Medal on the Dalai Lama, despite Beijing's strong opposition. That President George W. Bush handed the award to the Tibetan leader at a ceremony attended by Democratic and Republican luminaries and a host of celebrities added to Beijing's ire. Describing the move as "blatant interference" with China's internal affairs, a Foreign Ministry spokesman in Beijing said it had gravely undermined bilateral relations. The honour prompted some Tibetans to plan celebrations in Lhasa. The Chinese stepped by arresting the organisers, who included key monks. Over the months, protests to secure the release of those still in detention grew bigger. Beijing accused the Dalai Lama of masterminding the unrest to subvert the Beijing Olympics. Anti-Chinese demonstrations broke out in Tibet on March 10 on the 49th anniversary of the abortive uprising against Chinese rule.

In Kathmandu, Tibetans began staging daily protests in front of the Chinese Embassy, as the Nepalese security forces beat them back. Chinese ambassador Zheng Xianglin held a news conference to praise Nepalese police and denounce external forces for instigating violent activities against China.

While Maoist leader Dahal backed China's crackdown on the 'separatist violence' in Tibet, Nepalese officials became extra careful about western mountaineers heading to the Himalayas in the pre-Olympic phase to prevent unpleasant activities against the north. Beijing had closed its side of Mount Everest before the Olympic torch relay to the summit of the world's highest mountain to prevent demonstrations. It now asked Kathmandu to shut down access to southern climbing routes. Miffed that this was the high season for climbing in the Himalayas, which meant a loss of revenue, Nepal eventually agreed. It deported an American mountaineer intending to plant a Tibetan flag atop Mount Everest.

As reports of Chinese security agents in plain clothes directing the Nepalese suppression emerged, international human rights watchdog accused the Nepalese government of appeasing China. The fact that leaders who had overcome the royal regime's suppression now ordered similar action on the Tibetans was shocking. But the constituent assembly elections, delayed twice over internal political rifts, stood threatened by the burgeoning violence. After much behind-the-scenes negotiation, the Tibetans suspended their protests to allow the crucial elections to go forth. Chinese military publications stepped up anti-Indian rhetoric, calling the country 'arrogant' and warning it to stay away from a 'path of confrontation'. While not directly linking India to the Tibet unrest, the source of China's displeasure was clear enough.

Considering Nepal's important strategic location and the presence of many Tibetan refugees, Beijing felt inimical elements might take advantage of prolonged instability in Nepal. The open border with India and proximity to the Dalai Lama's base in the northern Indian city of Dharamshala had turned Nepal into a major transit point for Tibetans. Chinese analysts now spoke of Beijing's fear that Kathmandu might end up becoming a more radicalised version of Dharamshala. The possibility of Tibetan separatists entering the region through Nepal's northern border, much like the US Central Intelligence Agency-backed Khampa rebels in the 1960s, loomed larger in China's assessment.

If Beijing had grown increasingly distrustful of Nepalese authorities, Nepal's mainstream parties could not afford to undermine their credentials amid constant pressure from Western governments and international human rights organisations. The Maoist YCL had issued fiery threats against Tibetan protests organisers, but then vanished from the streets. Beijing had reason to suspect the YCL had become more deferential to Washington to ensure the withdrawal of the terrorist tag on the Maoists.

The Tibetan protests convinced Beijing of the futility of any understanding with New Delhi on minimising US interference, especially since the two countries had just signed a nuclear cooperation deal. From the wait-and-watch policy it had maintained in Nepal during much of 2006 and 2007, Beijing now began taking a more pragmatic stand towards the Maoists, while cultivating relations with the other major political forces, including Madhes-based parties.

Dubious Deadlock

CONVENING ON MAY 28, 2008, the constituent assembly voted 560-4 to finalise the abolition of Nepal's 240-year old Shah monarchy – but not before hours of suspense and anxiety. Originally scheduled to meet at 11 am, the crucial session was postponed by hours several times. Even at the late stage, some believed the military and traditional loyalists and possibly external powers having second thoughts after the Maoists' victory would step in to save the monarchy. Throughout the day, an anxious Maoist chief Pushpa Kamal Dahal sought regular updates from Prime Minister Girija Prasad Koirala on how developments could unfold. One witness reported seeing a confident Koirala reassuring Dahal not to worry as things were proceeding according to plan. The final result was announced close to midnight.

The suspense continued for another two weeks, as King Gyanendra consulted with advisers, military officers and government representatives on his next move. He had reinstated the House of Representatives on the understanding that monarchy would be part of the polity. From his perspective, the status quo had been restored to the night the legislature was dissolved in 2002. Restoring Sher Bahadur Deuba's elected government and the state of emergency to fight the Maoists militarily may have been out of the question in the prevailing circumstances. Yet the Constitution of 1990 was in operation and any effort to bring the Maoists on board would proceed under the system of king-in-parliament.

The mainstream parties and the Maoists had launched a movement to end an 'autocratic monarchy' to which the people had responded. Far from considering the monarchy as inherently autocratic and thus subject to outright removal, the protesters intended to restore the palace to its constitutional role. Yet the parties had sidelined and subsequently abolished the monarchy through a series of political decisions. The constituent assembly, elected in a process that systematically stifled pro-monarchy voices, was asked to formalise a decision that was inherently unconstitutional to begin with. Many Nepalese refused to believe someone crowned twice in exceptional circumstances would so easily consent to become a commoner. Even if he did, others wondered, would the monarch stay in Nepal or go into exile? In interviews, Dahal urged the former king to stay in the country and do something constructive as a citizen.

The premier-in-waiting was not only being magnanimous. So prominent a political figure with such powerful ambitions could pose a greater threat to the new system from abroad. Over the centuries, legions of Nepalese political exiles of all persuasions had established that. Dahal himself recognised how much the safety the Maoist leadership found on Indian soil had contributed to their latest triumph. With little to do at home, many average Nepalese believed the ex-monarch would go to India or the United Kingdom, two favourites destinations of Nepalese royals. Emerging to address the media, the former monarch made clear he was going to stay in Nepal. Shedding his customary royal vocabulary to reconcile with the new reality, the now Mr Gyanendra Shah addressed the Nepalese as 'brothers and sisters' before vacating the royal palace for the short drive to his private residence.

The next order of business was the election of a president. Instant disagreements surfaced between the mainstream parties and the Maoists over whether the head of state should be chosen by a simple or two-thirds majority of the constituent assembly. The Maoists, relenting to a simple majority, eventually also agreed to a ceremonial head of state instead of the powerful executive they had been advocating all along.

The next person to lose after the monarchy was outgoing Prime Minister Koirala. Unofficial reports suggested that Dahal had promised Koirala the presidency in recognition of his contributions to Nepal's sustained struggle for democracy. That honour would have been well deserved. Koirala had taken part in every democratic struggle since 1950. He was instrumental in the Nepali Congress's ability to maintain organisational sturdiness throughout the three decades it was officially banned. During that period, he also was at the forefront of reconciliation efforts between the palace and the Nepali Congress. While many Nepalese still held him personally responsible for the factionalism, nepotism and corruption that eroded Nepal's democratic experience in the 1990s, they also knew Koirala had lost none of his fighting zeal when he saw royal assertiveness imperilling democracy again.

A hardliner on the Maoists while in power, Koirala also had a degree of flexibility his personality and temperament often obscured. Maintaining a strong record of anti-communism, he had once worked comfortably with the monarchy before perceiving renewed royal machinations amid the outbreak of the Maoist insurgency in 1996. Years of disenchantment since had warmed him towards the Maoists.

The promise of the presidency was also thought to have partly contributed to Koirala's turn away from a ceremonial monarchy to full-fledged republicanism. However, Dahal now insisted that Koirala, at age 83, should not be burdened with the onerous responsibilities of the state. Koirala confidants, who initially lobbied New Delhi on his behalf, detected India's reluctance to see a powerful personality at the helm (Sharma, 2019).

An incensed Koirala delayed his resignation, fuelling Maoist suspicions and prompting far from gentle nudges from New Delhi. Together with the Madhesi Janadhikar Forum (MJF) – the other new force in electoral politics – the Maoists named as their presidential candidate Ramraja Prasad Singh, a Madhesi leader who once waged a violent campaign against the monarchy. At a public function, ambassador Sood was overheard congratulating Singh in advance. It had been utterly premature. The MJF subsequently joined the CPN-UML in backing Ram Baran Yadav, the Nepali Congress general secretary and a Madhesi. In return, the MJF candidate Parmanand Jha, a former Supreme Court justice, was elected vice-president. With the first elected head of state and his deputy both belonging to the Terai, Nepalese expected the process of reconciliation to ease.

With the Maoists poised to take the helm, expectations of an improvement in Sino-Nepalese relations grew. An influential Chinese newspaper described the Maoists' victory as "a historic sea change" that had left Washington worried that Kathmandu might tilt toward Beijing. Recalling that India and the U.S. both had designated the Maoists a "terrorist organisation," Beijing also sought to draw a favourable contrast by suggesting it had only called the group anti-government rebels. Citing New Delhi's announcement of its willingness to "unconditionally cooperate" with the Maoist government, the newspaper attributed the shift to Delhi's desire both to prevent Kathmandu from cosying up to Beijing and to dissuade the CPN-M from supporting Maoist insurgents in India (Upadhya, 2012).

Just after the elections, Beijing sent a nine-member official Foreign Ministry delegation to Nepal headed by Assistant Minister Ha Yafei. This followed reports of high-level meetings between Nepalese and Chinese officials on the government formation in Nepal. Beijing, according to one Chinese analyst, weighed two broad approaches and corresponding policy options: a) cultivate productive interaction with the ruling elites of the country and guarantee a preferable policy toward China; or follow an ideological course and seek workable ties with the Maoists (Zhang, 2006). China concluded the latter course neither realistic nor feasible, especially since it had long abandoned the practice of 'exporting' revolutions. The same pragmatic calculations now led Beijing to engage with the Maoists once they became part of the political mainstream.

Reflecting its residual embarrassment by the tactics the rebels used during the 'people's war', Beijing politely advised Dahal to drop the Maoist suffix from the organisation's name. They would be comfortable with anything symbolising 'Prachanda Path' – Dahal's synthesis of the principles of Marxism, Leninism and Maoism and the experiences of the first five years of the Nepalese insurgency. The Maoists declined (Lovell, 2019). In an interview with a Chinese newspaper, Dahal emphasised the geographic proximity between China and Nepal, and the high respect that the Nepalese people had for China and the Chinese people. He added: "For Nepal's national independence, it is critically important for Nepal to maintain intimate relations with China." Chiding Western-style capitalism, he praised China's model of economic development as one that Nepal would emulate (Hsiao, 2008).

China had more immediate worries, as Tibetan exiles resumed the protests they had suspended for the CA election. This time, Beijing expressed unhappiness over the Nepalese government's lacklustre efforts to control the demonstrations. Chinese ambassador Zheng publicly urged Kathmandu to take sterner action against the Tibetans involved in protests. He described the demonstrators as 'separatists' who were being supported by United Nations offices and human rights groups. Zheng said he was aware Nepal was under pressure from the international community over its attempts to stop the demonstrations, but added the current measures were not enough. "Arresting Tibetan demonstrators and releasing them hours later is nothing but a drama," he said.

THE CONSTITUENT ASSEMBLY finally elected Dahal as prime minister on August 15. After significant political wrangling, he formed a cabinet with the CPN-UML's Bam Dev Gautam as deputy prime minister and home minister, the Maoists' chief ideologue Baburam Bhattarai as finance minister, and the MJF's Upendra Yadav as foreign minister. The Maoists were anxious to play down suggestions of an impending pro-Chinese tilt. Dahal insisted that Nepal would maintain a foreign policy of equidistance with Nepal's two neighbours, while acknowledging Nepal's deep "civilisational and cultural ties" with India. He praised as "instrumental" India's role in bringing about the 12-point understanding between the alliance of seven parties and the Maoists, an exercise that remained shrouded in much mystery. Yet Dahal's deputy in the party, Bhattarai, widely considered the most India-friendly Maoist leader, continued to maintain that the open border prevented Nepal from achieving economic prosperity.

Before the internal ramifications of the new political equation in power could be properly gauged, Dahal triggered a row with India by deciding to attend the closing ceremony of the Beijing Olympics. That otherwise innocuous move broke with the tradition of Nepalese prime ministers first visiting India in acknowledgement of the exceptionally close bilateral ties. In Beijing, Dahal held extensive talks with President Hu Jintao and Premier Wen Jiabao in what had become an official visit in all but name. He promised to continue to clamp down on 'free Tibet' activities on Nepalese soil, which had become Beijing's major source of concern.

Dahal's China visit enthused the nationalist constituency – including many on the royalist right – and enervated influential sections in India. Barely had Dahal landed home than he went on full damage-control mode. Nepal's neighbourhood policy was not a zero-sum game, the Maoist leader insisted. Exhibiting his insurgency-era capacity for linguistic legerdemain, Dahal said he would make his first political visit to India.

Honouring that pledge in mid-September, Dahal reiterated to his host that he had maintained tradition because his Beijing visit was unofficial. New Delhi, letting go of the fact that Dahal had been flaunting the China visit as a major part of his government's 'discontinuity' with past Nepalese regimes, gave him a warm welcome. Yet the past continued to cast a shadow on events. An embankment breach on the Kosi River flooded a large area of Nepal's eastern Terai region, displacing around 65,000 people and affecting up to two million Indians. India, which had built the embankment, oversaw maintenance. New Delhi complained that the lack of cooperation at the local level had prevented necessary repairs. Both countries agreed to discuss future arrangements for resolving such bilateral issues.

The Maoists' history of fierce anti-Indianism, not to mention traditional Nepalese scepticism of their giant southern neighbour, did not stop Dahal from mounting a charm offensive on the Indian leadership across the ideological spectrum. Emerging from talks with his counterpart, Dr Manmohan Singh, and other senior leaders, Dahal spoke of a new beginning in relations. Curiously, he did so by circuitously reviving the term 'special relations' that had marred them in the past. By winning New Delhi's firm commitment on a thorough review of the 1950 Treaty of Peace and Friendship and other agreements, Dahal gained a major symbolic victory. By the time the joint statement came out, the tricky text had imposed stern responsibilities on the man once known as the Fierce One.

The Indian media became ever more euphoric as they discovered new facets of the once shadowy leader who some never believed really existed. Entrenched adversaries like leaders of the Bharatiya Janata Party, which resented Dahal for his ideology, were charmed by his invocation of Lord Pashupatinath. The premier disowned all but ideological ties with the Indian Maoists, who, according to Singh, posed the most significant internal security challenge for India since independence. Dahal used his interactions with India Inc. to demolish Maoist shibboleths, a turnaround that must have astounded even the Great Helmsman's reformist successors in Beijing.

Sceptics saw Dahal in a chameleon-like avatar, ready to assume colours appropriate to his audience. The Maoists could demand a revisit of Nepal's Sugauli Treaty (1816) with British India. In that case, Nepal could lay claims to almost half of Himachal Pradesh, all of Uttarakhand, Sikkim and Darjeeling. In 2005, Baburam Bhattarai had stated that Nepal could never develop until the territories lost by the treaty were restored. During his press conference in New Delhi the following year, Dahal categorically emphasised the need to review the various 'unequal' bilateral treaties, including the Friendship Treaty of 1950 between India and Nepal (Nayak, 2007). Overall, though, Dahal focused enough attention on himself to leave India firmly glued to his government's next move. That was fast in coming, with China granting $1.3 million in military aid during Defence Minister Ram Bahadur Thapa's visit to Beijing. By then, Dahal had embarked on a global performance.

In terms of sheer symbolism, the prime minister's visit to the United States capped it all. Although technically a trip to address the United Nations General Assembly, Washington seemed quite anxious to make a close appraisal of the watch-and-wait policy it had adopted since the Maoists emerged as the largest party in the April elections. That President George W. Bush invited the leader of an organisation still listed on one of Washington's terrorist lists to his traditional reception for visiting heads of state and government was telling enough. The brief exchange of words between Bush and Dahal confirming continued cooperation marked a victory for the Maoists. When junior State Department officials met the premier, they were clearly seeking to set the parameters for an eventual full rapprochement.

In his address to the UN assembly, Dahal attempted to cast his party's decade-long bloody insurgency as a national liberation movement, using other public forums on the sidelines to unveil his vision for the future. Within a month of his rise to power, the three principal external stakeholders had established Dahal's credibility as a partner. Eager for more, the premier reached out to Russia for military assistance, almost seeking to entice a resurgent Moscow back to a Cold War-era role in Nepal.

International success did not necessarily solidify a leader's internal flank. In resource-starved Nepal, the flamboyance of the premier abroad, not the prospect of enhanced global goodwill, became the news. The possible political ramifications for the ruling coalition, a fractious amalgamation at best, began consuming the punditocracy and people alike. Nepal badly needed a strong and efficient post-monarchy government, lest the experiment embarrass the purveyors of novelty.

Despite their mutual distrust lingering from the abortive alliance on the presidential election, the Maoists, CPN-UML and MJF had made the best deal possible within the internal and geopolitical dynamics. During Dahal's absence, however, the bad blood between Deputy Prime Minister Gautam and Finance Minister Bhattarai over ministerial protocol spilt out in the open. The protests sparked by the new budget's slashing of funds for traditional religious observances did much more than pit Gautam and Bhattarai on opposite sides. How an officially secular state would sustain rituals and festivals defining the Nepalese character under a government led by an ideologically atheist party began boggling more and more minds on the eve of the Dasain festival.

Structurally, the government had enough ingredients to implode. The CPN-UML and the MJF had exhorted their youth cadres to go after the Maoist Young Communist League (YCL). By continuing to oppose the merger of the People's Liberation Army (PLA) with the Nepal Army in ever stronger terms, the MJF had raised the stakes several notches. The move may have cheered the army, intent on preserving its professionalism, but it also cast a shadow on a key component underpinning the peace process.

The Terai Madhes Loktantrik Party, for its part, had demanded full consultations with its constituents before the government revised the 1950 treaty. Considering how closely the treaty influenced everyday life in the region bordering India, the demand was valid. Operationally, achieving a national consensus on the precise changes Nepal was seeking and calibrating them with New Delhi's obvious preference for comprehensiveness would be daunting enough. Fusing the Terai's aspirations and expectations into the national agenda could leave Nepal scribbling several drafts, especially now that over a dozen armed groups active in the region were veering toward some form of unity.

For Dahal, the real siege lay within. Land Reforms Minister Matrika Yadav's antics and his subsequent resignation only exemplified the rifts within the Maoists. The controversy sparked by the Maoists' bearing arms in public places, including the CA premises, drew clear battle lines. A strong constituency among the former rebels was resentful of Dahal's apparent readiness to dilute the ideological wholesomeness of the struggle in the name of political expediency. Further clashes between rival factions, while still sporadic, could increase amid deepening polarisation. While the fractured nature of the popular mandate had stymied the Maoists, Dahal's eagerness to gain legitimacy from the foreign powers he spent years denouncing was more liable to be seen as capitulation than conciliation.

All this redounded to the benefit of the Nepali Congress. Having abandoned its longstanding support for the monarchy, exposing itself to a communist juggernaut, the party was desperate for a revival strategy. Despite the official reunification of the party, members of both factions had candidly acknowledged the lack of emotional unity. The Nepali Congress immediately pounced on Dahal's and other Maoist leaders' reiteration that they did not support traditional parliamentary democracy for Nepal. For an organisation that had raised arms against both the monarchy and parliamentary democracy, the Maoists' desire to radically restructure the polity evidently reflected the aspirations of a strong segment of the rank and file. Many Nepalese disenchanted by the 1990-2002 democratic era, too, were understandably eager for something new. Yet Dahal's failure to articulate the precise nature of a middle path had undercut his repudiation of a one-party state replacing the monarchy.

CPN-UML general secretary Jhal Nath Khanal, as a major critic of the People's Multiparty Democracy doctrine that mainstreamed his once-radical communist faction, was inclined to inject revolutionary fervour among cadres. His qualified endorsement of a non-traditional democracy under the new Constitution was partly aimed for internal consumption. The public convergence of the two communist parties' disavowal of conventional democracy had given the Nepali Congress the cover to deflect public attention from its internal woes to the purported threat the country once again confronted.

Significantly, the first salvo was fired by a Maoist-friendly leader Shekhar Koirala, who warned that his party could pull out of the assembly en masse to protest any Maoist tilt towards totalitarianism. NC vice-president Ram Chandra Poudel equated Dahal's stance with that of King Mahendra while dismissing Nepal's first elected government and abolishing parliamentary democracy in 1960.

NC president Koirala, insisting that the contradictions within the coalition would be enough to bring it down, promised his party would discharge the role of a responsible opposition and focus on drafting the new Constitution on time. Judging by the party's – and Koirala's – past, it was hard to see it desisting from any effort that would hasten that collapse.

Having kept the party intact during its massive battlefield and political setbacks during the insurgency, Dahal needed to prove he could steer the ship in new turbulent waters. Although more militant members had formed another group, vowing to continue the people's war, the split had not been that grievous. Dahal, however, could no longer expect to play the hardliners and moderates off against each other. Whether in power or out, he would come under greater pressure to either bridge the two or pick a side. Either way, he was unlikely to emerge unscathed.

As New Delhi shared those concerns, the Chinese were driven to adjust their policy on Nepal. The Tibetans' protest during the two previous years had impelled Beijing cultivate the Maoists. By the end of 2008, after the waves of anti-Chinese demonstrations by Tibetans, Beijing replaced its ambassador Zheng in Kathmandu with Qiu Guohong, deputy director of the Asian Affairs of the Ministry of Foreign Affairs. That was a prelude to a wider jockeying for influence in the triangular relationship.

Deputy Prime Minister Gautam urged China to help Nepal resolve its long-running dispute with India over the territory of Kalapani. Indian Foreign Minister Pranab Mukherjee, signalling India's displeasure, did not meet with Gautam during his visit a few days later. Shortly after Mukherjee's departure, Chinese Foreign Minister Yang Jiechi arrived in Kathmandu undertaking to develop bilateral relations based on 'real equality' so that it could become a 'role model' for relationships between big and small countries. At an official dinner, Yang pledged China's help to Nepal in its effort to strengthen its sovereignty and independence. The statement prompted questions in the legislature whether that offer came in response to any request from Dahal.

Former king Gyanendra was quoted in an interview as saying that his policy of moving closer towards China had brought about his downfall, clearly indicating that it had angered India. A discomfited Chinese ambassador Qiu Guohong praised the monarchy's contributions to fostering bilateral relations, while adding that Beijing respected the choice of the Nepalese people.

But he was evasive on the deputy prime minister's request for Beijing's involvement in resolving the Kalapani dispute. That scarcely mollified India, concerned by the flurry of senior Chinese officials landing in Kathmandu.

The Madhesi movement had provided new urgency to Beijing, which saw it as part of a design to establish a powerful Madhes province that would be soft towards New Delhi and dilute the influence of the traditional Kathmandu-based power elite. China saw that eventuality ultimately aimed against itself. Describing the events unfolding in the Madhes as 'unnatural and extraordinary', China's top expert on Nepal said they were being orchestrated to destabilise Nepal (Wang, 2007). Few among his fraternity felt the need to name India.

In early 2009, Dahal's Maoists united with a smaller communist party to officially become the United Communist Party of Nepal-Maoist (UCPN-Maoist). Addressing a public rally, Dahal said the unification heralded a "new era in the fight against imperialism" and lambasted entities who would interfere with the Maoists' control of the government, indirectly including his coalition partners. In office, however, the Maoists did not seek to implement the radical policies they had pushed during the decade-long insurgency, such as land redistribution, socialist economics, and nationalisation.

The Maoist leadership appeared flexible enough to work with the other parties in open and competitive politics. Many cadres, however, were already becoming wary of compromises the leadership was making. Integrating the two armies remained an obstacle to the peace process. Mainstream parties saw that a precondition to a healthy space capable of accommodating the Maoists and other political actors. However, the Maoists feared that without their army, rival political parties might try to marginalise them.

General Discontent

At the core were the different interpretations by the Nepal Army and the Maoists of the ambiguous wording of the 2006 Comprehensive Peace Agreement (CPA) and other documents on the modalities for integration. While the Maoists wanted to integrate their armed cadres en masse into the national army, the generals wanted the ex-rebel soldiers limited to civilian work or accommodated into the police services. The Nepali Congress and MJF and external powers such as India and the United States also opposed collective integration of Maoist fighters into the national army. Relations between the Maoists and the generals, already sour over the army's resumption of recruitment, deteriorated when Defence Minister Thapa – a former Maoist commander – refused to extend the appointments of eight brigadier generals. (The Supreme Court eventually reinstated them.)

The Maoists raised the stakes in May by trying to remove army chief, Gen. Rookmangud Katawal, a leading commander in the royal regime's anti-Maoist campaign, months before he was set to retire. The government appointed his second-in-command, Lt.-Gen. Kul Bahadur Khadka, who was to retire before Gen. Katawal. Non-Maoist parties suspected that Dahal had brokered a deal with Gen. Khadka under which he would act in their interest in return for the promotion. Responding to an appeal by 18 political parties represented in the constituent assembly, President Ram Baran Yadav urged Gen. Katawal to continue in office, arguing that he, as supreme commander-in-chief, had not been consulted. The president's critics hit back, saying a titular head of state lacked the power to override cabinet decisions. In a surprising move, Dahal resigned as prime minister the following day, decrying what he called the president's violation of civilian supremacy. In a televised speech, Dahal declared he would not stay in office bowing before 'foreign forces' in a thinly veiled reference to India.

Later reports suggested that Indian leaders had urgently telephoned key Nepalese counterparts to press Yadav to overrule the decision because of the traditional relationship between the two militaries. Moreover, Indian officials insisted that, during Dahal's visit to India, they had pressed the Maoists not to interfere with the Nepal Army structure or personnel (Jha, 2012). New Delhi saw the sacking as part of a calibrated indirect move by Beijing to extend its influence on Nepal's military in advance of Dahal's imminent second visit to China. That Dahal and Beijing had tried to use India's preoccupation with the elections had exacerbated those concerns.

Of the near dozen high-level Chinese delegations visiting Nepal in 2008-2009, two were military teams. A week after Foreign Minister Yang Jiechi's visit, Lt-Gen Ma Xiaotian, deputy chief of General Staff of the Chinese PLA, led a ten-member delegation with a pledge of $2.61 million worth of security assistance. Two months later, a second high-level PLA delegation arrived. Moreover, China had proposed a revised draft of the bilateral Peace and Friendship Treaty of 1960, ostensibly intending to match it with the treaty Nepal had signed with India a decade earlier. In proposing the draft, Foreign Minister Yang also talked about "all kinds of Chinese assistance to help Nepal safeguard its sovereignty and territorial integrity". Chinese Assistant Foreign Minister Hu Zhengyue visited Kathmandu on 26 February and handed over the draft to Nepal's acting foreign secretary Suresh Pradhan.

Like his boss, Foreign Minister Upendra Yadav, head of the MJF, was positive about the treaty. A high-level Chinese delegation had participated in the general convention of Yadav's party in Birgunj. Preparations were afoot to sign the new treaty in Beijing during Dahal's scheduled trip to China from May 2. The two countries planned to open up additional border points and bring Chinese railways and roads up to the border. Talks were also progressing on Chinese aid to build a hydropower plant in a hilly district and in opening an agricultural university in Chitwan, respectively a sector and a region India traditionally considered its preserve.

The other elements of the bilateral agenda – a five-point memorandum of understanding on economic and technical cooperation, a study to upgrade the ring road in Kathmandu, a dry port at Tatopani, vehicles and equipment for solid waste management, and exchange of youth delegations – promised to raise Nepal-China relations to a new level. Amid the pressure building around the Katawal controversy, however, Dahal informed Chinese ambassador Qiu Guohong that he was suspending the visit (Sharma, 2019).

The Chinese found the Maoist-led government and former guerrilla cabinet ministers easy to work with because they had no preoccupations about democracy or freedom of the press. The Chinese were especially impressed with the Maoists' firm stand in quelling pro-Tibet protests. The 2008 Olympic protests occurred during a Congress-led government in Nepal. When the Maoists came into power in June, they clamped down on Tibetans in Kathmandu by pre-emptively arresting protesters before the Dalai Lama's birthday and the anniversary of Tibet annexation (Dixit, 2010).

India's direct interference in what was essentially an internal civilian-military conflict would have enduring ramifications for the Sino-Indian rivalry over shaping the country's new polity. In later comments, Dahal would blame bureaucratic bungling by New Delhi and call for greater engagement between the two countries' political leaders to prevent such misunderstanding in the future. Yet Dahal also continued to project – especially to the party faithful – his departure as the price he had to pay for trying to build closer relations with China.

The constituent assembly elected Madhav Kumar Nepal of the CPN-UML as the prime minister on May 23, 2009. Enjoying the support of 22 parties, including the Nepali Congress, Nepal was known as a soft-spoken consensus builder. However, his election was dogged by questions of legitimacy arising from his defeat from two constituencies in the election. Complicating matters, the MJF split as the new government was being formed. The Nepal government enjoyed strong support from India primarily because New Delhi saw it as the best way to keep the Maoists out of power and correct its pro-Chinese course.

While Prime Minister Singh's United Progressive Alliance fell a dozen short of a majority in the recent election, it no longer had to rely on the support of the Marxists, which had led New Delhi's effort to mainstream the Maoists. Sceptics of the 2005-2006 process were replacing elements in the Indian bureaucracy and intelligence services considered soft on the Nepalese Maoists. Persisting with his rhetoric attacks on New

Delhi, Dahal nevertheless maintained contacts with Indian academics and intelligence agents, mostly in Singapore and London. New Delhi was insistent on preventing the Maoists' return to power before they instituted a 'course correction'. In other words, the Maoists had to convince India of their commitment to democracy, marginalise those who New Delhi considered the more troublesome elements in the party, stop hobnobbing with China, and abandon their military wing (Jha 2014). Yet New Delhi was also keen on maintaining back channels.

Indian suspicions were raised when they discovered that Dahal was also meeting with Chinese representatives in Hong Kong and the mainland. Chinese concern had intensified around this time when six CA members belonging to Madhesi parties travelled to Dharamshala in India to meet the Dalai Lama and made comments linking Tibetan independence with the struggle for Madhesi autonomy (Sharma, 2019). Although the meeting was said to have been arranged by a private foundation, the Nepalese legislators raised the stakes by inviting the Tibetan leader to visit Nepal. The Dalai Lama conceded that despite his longstanding desire to visit the country, successive Nepalese governments could not invite him because of sustained Chinese pressure (Upadhya, 2012).

As Prime Minister Nepal travelled to India on a goodwill visit, Nepalese security and law-enforcement officials held talks in Lhasa with their Chinese counterparts on securing the border and cracking down on anti-Tibet activities. Beijing characterised demands for a separate autonomous northern region in eastern Nepal, pushed by ethnic activists, as a Western-funded effort to promote anti-Tibet activities. Of the

14 Nepalese districts bordering Tibet, China considered eight sensitive and sought tougher measures from local authorities.

China's urgency had been heightened by fresh clashes in Xinjiang autonomous region involving ethnic Uighurs and Han Chinese, which left over 150 dead, triggering an outcry from human-rights organisations and exiled groups. Beijing feared the possibility of wider instability in the region bordering Tibet. The government announced a ban on anti-Chinese protests but clarified that the Dalai Lama was free to visit the country as long as he did not pursue a political agenda.

Premier Nepal went on to address the United Nations in September, but attention was already focused on how Beijing viewed him. During one point in the anti-palace agitation, Nepal had strongly criticised China for arming the royal regime against the people. His accusation was doubly stinging for Beijing since he had made them during a visit to India. Among the new premier's early affirmations was that Nepal did not intend to play China off against India and sought to project a balanced relationship. In September, Zhang Gaoli, a member of the politburo of the Chinese Communist Party Central Committee, arrived on a five-day visit to Kathmandu at the invitation of the government. During the visit, the highest level of its kind since the post-2006 political changes, Zhang met with President Ram Baran Yadav, Prime Minister Nepal, and the leaders of the major political parties.

In a key speech in Kathmandu, Zhang – acknowledged by a leading Nepalese analyst as China's most senior fifth-generation leader, and a leading candidate to succeed the successor of President Hu Jintao – observed that "we have always treated our relations with Nepal from a strategic high and with a long-term view." He thanked the government and people of Nepal for their sympathy and understanding on Tibet, Xinjiang and other issues of vital importance to China. Yet in his private meetings, he, too, was reported to have sought greater action from Nepal on curbing anti-China activities. Zhang was also reported to have advised the Maoists and the CPN-UML to forge unity to "match the forces that were inimical to China" (Upadhya, 2010).

Kathmandu sought to address some of Beijing's concerns by announcing it would soon deploy thousands of armed police along the Himalayan border, carefully asserting that it was not acting under pressure from Beijing. But the urgency on the part of the Chinese was unmistakable. The biennial defence white paper for 2008 for the first time listed "separatists … working for the independence of Tibet" as a national security threat. Some 2,500 Tibetans made the dangerous trip from Tibet to Nepal every year on their way to India to join the Dalai Lama. Activists said that number had fallen sharply since China mobilised its military in Tibet in March 2008. Official Nepalese reaffirmations of its "one China" policy had become tediously repetitive since the abolition of the monarchy, yet Beijing's pressure on Kathmandu only seemed to mount. Were the Chinese using the Tibet issue to pursue a broader agenda in Nepal?

Maoist leader Dahal helped deflect that question by claiming that India and the United States had been plotting serious anti-China activities from Nepal, including even an attack on China, an assertion that prompted ridicule from New Delhi. Still, the allegation came amid a flurry of visits by western and Chinese ambassadors to Mustang, the one-time base of the Khampa rebellion. Rumours that Tibetan leaders from India had also visited the north-western Nepalese region added an ominous chord to the discourse.

Dahal visited Hong Kong for what the Maoists officially described was a meeting with Nepalese supporters in the Chinese territory. The Nepalese media reported in substantial detail how the Maoist leader was whisked away from the airport for a secret meeting with unnamed Chinese officials who had flown in from Beijing. In October, the Maoist leader revisited China, this time heading an eight-member delegation of his party. It held four rounds of talks with CCP members. President Hu Jintao hosted Dahal as the guest of honour at the country's 11th National Games in Shandong and met with him privately for 25 minutes. Chinese sources insisted that Hu and Dahal had met as leaders of their countries' communist parties to inaugurate inter-party ties, which had not been possible during Dahal's previous visit as prime minister.

The Dalai Lama's visit to the north-eastern Indian state of Arunachal Pradesh in November prompted a strong denunciation from Beijing, which claims the region as southern Tibet. By raising tensions in the disputed region, according to one Chinese analyst, New Delhi hoped to force Beijing to resolve the issue on its terms. Weeks earlier, Beijing had lodged a vehement protest when Prime Minister Manmohan Singh visited the state during an election campaign.

After Dahal's return from China, the Maoists ratcheted up their rhetorical campaign against India. In one public speech, Dahal virtually accused New Delhi of masterminding the murders of King Birendra and the CPN-UML's charismatic general secretary Madan Bhandari, who died in a mysterious car accident in 1993. While such allegations were nothing new in Nepal's tiresome political discourse, this was the first time such a senior political leader had made them.

During a visit to China in late December, Prime Minister Nepal reaffirmed Nepal's traditional one China policy. To underscore his commitment, the premier had begun the visit from Tibet. Beijing, which now considered Kathmandu's Tibet policy a litmus test of its professions of friendship, appreciated the gesture. As the first prime minister of republican Nepal officially visiting China, his arrival in Beijing carried its own significance. The size and content of the joint statement the two countries subsequently issued provided another indication of the direction relations would take. Nepal and China agreed to lift their bilateral relationship to a higher level by establishing a "comprehensive partnership of cooperation". In his meeting with the Nepalese premier, China's top legislator Wu Bangguo was more candid: the objective of the comprehensive partnership was 'strategic'. Over the next few weeks, Chinese analysts would emphasise the importance of small border states adjoining India and China to Chinese security. One asserted that the struggle between pro-India and pro-China forces in Nepal had reached a critical stage and that China needed to pay more attention to its interests there.

The United States, which had largely followed India's lead during the second term of President Bush and first year of the Obama administration, now seemed to chart a middle ground. During his confirmation hearings in the Senate, the American ambassador-designate, Scott DeLisi, acknowledged China as a stakeholder on par with India in Nepal, an assertion he repeated after assuming his responsibilities in Kathmandu. Washington and Beijing also held subregional consultations on South Asia in the Chinese capital. This brought them closer to the European view that the Maoists could no longer be isolated from power if Nepal were to achieve lasting peace and stability. While some Indians sulked at the loss of their initiative in Nepal, others were aware of the negative fallout from any precipitate overt action. But the window of opportunity was narrowing. The threat of a serious political crisis loomed large as the assembly appeared certain to miss the deadline for drafting the new constitution.

After much last-minute posturing, the Maoists voted in favour of extending the constituent assembly for a year after receiving what they believed was an assurance of resignation from Prime Minister Nepal. Hopes that the political parties had finally created space to sort out their difficulties faltered as the Maoists accused the ruling coalition of betrayal. Prime Minister Nepal, backed by the Nepali Congress, refused to resign until the Maoists demonstrated their commitment to turn into a fully disarmed and transparent political party.

The Indian government, as the prime facilitator of the peace process, had become increasingly apprehensive in public over the fraying of consensus, a sentiment broadly shared by other key governments. UN Secretary-General Ban Ki-moon stepped forth with incredible frankness on the roadblocks he saw. With time running out for the parties to draft and promulgate the new Constitution – the culmination of a process inaugurated amid much optimism – the all-round apprehension was entirely reasonable. A popularly drafted Constitution remained Nepal's best hope of acquiring the political stability central to the sustenance of a 'new' Nepal. Having averaged one basic law per decade, Nepalese had paid a heavy cumulative price for political improvisation.

Still, the key protagonists were digging in their heels deeper. Each instance of Maoist obstructionism had prompted disdain from the Nepali Congress and the CPN-UML, which, in turn, had ratcheted up tensions. Forebodings of a 'political accident' invariably went with every utterance in favour of amity. Part of the reason was that the peace process remained deeply flawed. After the collapse of royal rule, the Nepali Congress, and, specifically, then-prime minister Koirala, made all-out efforts to accede to every demand the Maoists made. Since it was crucial to keep the Maoists tied deep into the process, ambiguities and outright prevarications underpinned what essentially became periodic adjustments of disagreements. The goalposts were shifted every step of the way, but the players ultimately could accept the rules under the rubric of advancing the peace process.

With the monarchy out of the way, the political parties were expected to turn against one other. But the rivalries had turned far worse. The Nepali Congress and the CPN-UML seemed incapable of reconciling to the fact that Maoists had emerged as the largest party in mostly free and fair elections. The Maoists, despite lacking a majority, appeared convinced of almost a divine right to rule.

The political class's inability to figure out who nudged whom along the path towards a 'new' Nepal had been troubling enough. The geopolitical manoeuvrings precipitated by the vacuum left behind by the monarchy had worsened matters. The palace, for all the internal calumnies it drew, at least enjoyed enough confidence of the principal external stakeholders to guarantee stability on that vital front. Once in power, the Maoists overplayed their hand by seeking to shift Nepal's geopolitical locus northward to the point of utter defiance. This, more than anything else, hastened their fall from power. If not the sacking and subsequent reinstatement of the chief of the army staff, then some other controversy would have exposed the impossible strains that government straddled.

The collapse of the Maoist government set the stage for the next anomaly, i.e., the preponderance of people defeated in the elections serving in key posts in the new cabinet. The idea of fostering peace at all costs, noble though it was, would go on to exact its own price during the turbulent transition. Having failed in their crusade for 'civilian supremacy', the Maoists zeroed in on popular disenchantment. They demanded a national government and relaxed their stalling tactics in the constituent assembly. As the Nepali Congress and the CPN-UML rejoiced in what they saw as the Maoists' capitulation after months of swagger, the ex-rebels assured cadres of total state capture. The Maoists were relishing an influx of cadres from the CPN-UML, almost oblivious to the reality that they themselves were haemorrhaging to rival factions. The deep rifts within the CPN-UML seemed too delicious an opportunity for the Maoists to ignore. Prime Minister Nepal had become more outspoken about the lack of cooperation from the CPN-UML than from the ex-rebels.

The Nepali Congress, too, remained in a state of malaise. Koirala's decision to send daughter Sujata as the leader of the party's team in the cabinet and Ram Chandra Poudel's defeat of Sher Bahadur Deuba in the parliamentary party elections had set off a realignment process inherently different from the one that had characterised much of the post-1990 Nepali Congress. How events played out would become clearer after further spasms. The Maoists were no doubt keen to exploit rifts across the board. By accusing the Nepali Congress and the CPN-UML of having engineered the split in the MJF, the ex-rebels cleverly picked sides in an organisation that did much to erode their base in the Terai.

Amid all this gloom, the central truth of Nepal's political evolution had come out starker. Every political turn touted as a triumph had left the country progressively weaker. The triumph of the people had been hailed, only to pave the way for recognition that change had been incomplete. Yet internally, amid the effort to elaborate group grievances, there was a real danger of unleashing a process of fragmentation in perpetuity. Whether a constellation of microstates could be sustainable between two giant neighbours worried India and China more than it did Nepal.

China enjoyed an ethnic homogeneity that allowed for conformity on issues of national interest regardless of the polity in existence. In India, a remarkably diverse array of states had crafted a union rooted in consensual national objectives and policies. The recent upsurge in the fiery rhetoric between the two confident giants could only bode ill for a country so precariously perched in the middle. The imponderables presented by farther-flung powers – both in their official and non-government manifestations – had complicated Nepal's internal dynamics.

Moreover, a clear divergence was becoming evident in the perceptions and expectations from the peace process inside the country and outside. Even among external stakeholders, the struggle to carve spheres of influence was palpable. In a moment of remarkable forthrightness, CPN-UML chairman Jhal Nath Khanal claimed the new Constitution might end up being a "brochure of the agreements reached between the political parties, and thus incomplete".

The Constitution-writing schedule had already been changed seven times as key committees formed to deliberate on various sections and propose drafts, had yet to complete or submit their reports. The Maoists continued to block the proceedings of the constituent assembly to protest the president's move to reinstate the army chief. The constituent assembly was created to write the basic law and concurrently serve as parliament, which had exacerbated the delay. The people began worrying that a handful of people might hurriedly write the Constitution – if they did so at all within the two-year deadline set by the interim statute.

Two key issues – whether the executive system would be parliamentary or presidential and the model of federalism – continued to impede the process. Those disenchanted by Nepal's parliamentary history favoured the presidential system. Others worried that a presidential system could turn autocratic and undermine the legislature and judiciary. The debate on federalism revolved around whether to grant autonomy to ethnic communities and, if so, how much. The rightist parties and the dominant groups such as Bahun, Chhetri, and some upper caste Newars opposed significant autonomy.

In contrast, marginalised ethnic groups such as the Tharus, Limbus, Khambus, Tamangs, and regional identity groups like the Madhesis insisted on it. Although the Maoists had consistently supported the minority groups, many now believed they might give up ethnic autonomy in return for other priorities and spark new unrest. As a compromise, the CPN-UML favoured configuring regions around concentrations of major ethnic groups.

The Nepali Congress had accepted the integration of former Maoist guerrillas into the national army in earlier discussions. Now the party joined the MJF in opposing that, leading to disputes in October over the composition of the inter-party committee to resolve the issue. The mandate of the United Nations Mission in Nepal, whose functions included assisting with army integration, was renewed twice for six-month periods in January and again in July. It requested another extension at the end of the year.

Controversy continued over the lands the Maoists had seized during the insurgency. Despite frequent Maoist promises to return these plots, local cadres held on to them pending the 'scientific land reform' they had originally pledged to implement. State authority continued to erode in many local areas and a plethora of groups stepped into the vacuum. Within the left, serious clashes erupted between members of the Maoist YCL and the CPN-UML Youth Force. Ethnic Limbu organisations were running a parallel government in the eastern hills.

The most serious challenge to the peace process came from the assortment of armed groups in the Terai that had rejected the elections. Fourteen such groups met in the bordering Indian state of Bihar in September but failed to forge a common platform. As the government renewed its invitation for talks, many Nepalese began wondering whether they could have met across the border without Indian complicity.

By the end of 2009, when talks with India had broken

down, Dahal started accusing the Madhav Nepal government as an 'Indian puppet'. However, the Maoists had also sought to regain the initiative through fresh protests, demanding a national government under their leadership as the largest party in the constituent assembly. They also declared 13 autonomous ethnic and regional states. Conscious of the need to regain power to avoid irrelevance, the Maoists obstructed the legislature and threatened to bring a no-confidence motion against the Madhav Nepal government. Lacking support from other parties, Dahal launched an indefinite nationwide strike to force the prime minister's resignation. They were compelled to withdraw the strike a week later as Kathmandu residents resisted.

Girija Prasad Koirala's death in March 2010 at 86, marked the end of an era and brought a moment of unity. However, sustained pressure from the Maoists forced Madhav Nepal to resign at the end of June. Elections for a new prime minister were inconclusive over several months, preventing the government from passing a new budget. That slowed down state operations and development projects amid the growing power vacuum at the local level.

The Maoists and the Nepal Army continued to maintain diverging interpretations of how to integrate their respective forces. The Nepal Army insisted on limited integration. Few PLA members would be allowed into the army. They could not join as units or be given command positions. That went against what the Maoists had envisaged. Starting in January 2010, UNMIN disqualified over 4,000 PLA combatants (including child soldiers and individuals recruited after the cut-off date) and discharged them from cantonments. These disqualified combatants threatened to take up arms again if the government did not provide for their future livelihoods.

The deadlock goaded Nepal's two neighbours into action. In August, former foreign secretary Shyam Saran arrived in Kathmandu as Prime Minister Singh's special envoy. Known as the principal architect of the April 2006 revolution, Saran said Singh was concerned with Nepal's current political instability and had sent him to facilitate consensus. However, many Nepalese saw his arrival as part of New Delhi's effort to nudge Madhesi parties away from supporting Dahal's return to power and gauge the Maoists' willingness to engage with India. Saran was seen as someone enjoying excellent rapport with most Madhesi lawmakers and perhaps the only key member of India's Nepal policy team still with moderate views on the Maoists. He flew back to New Delhi as parliament failed to elect a premier a fourth time.

A month later, a delegation of 21 senior Chinese leaders led by Vice Premier He Yong arrived in Kathmandu on a six-day visit. This was the highest-level Chinese delegation to visit Nepal since the beginning of the peace process. The visit coincided with news of an audiotape purportedly containing a conversation between Krishna Bahadur Mahara, international bureau chief of the UCPN-Maoist and an unidentified Chinese. In the recording, Mahara was heard asking for 500 million rupees to buy off 50 lawmakers required to form the government under Dahal's leadership. If authentic, the tape indicated a serious shift in Chinese policy, which had traditionally shunned interference in Nepal's politics and castigated India for doing so. That caveat was a big one, especially amid reports that RAW had leaked the recording on the eve of the sixth round of voting. Realising that India would not allow him to be prime minister, Dahal withdrew his candidacy (Sharma, 2019).

The Chinese delegation's arrival also came amid a souring of relations between Beijing and New Delhi over China's denial of visa to a senior Indian general, stapled visas being issued to Kashmiris, and China's claim on Arunachal Pradesh. Beijing and New Delhi were now competing for influence along the Nepal-China border. After India provided Rs. 100 million in assistance for the remote hill region of Mustang, China responded with Rs. 10 million to construct a library, science laboratory and a computer-equipped school building in the region. The Indian and Chinese ambassadors both visited the area. Along Nepal's border with India, Beijing set up China Study Centres. In response to China's effort to extend the railway link from Tibet to the Nepalese border, India was contemplating rail links to its border with Nepal.

In mid-September, the government and Maoists agreed to complete the remaining tasks of the peace process by January 14, 2011, and extended UNMIN for four months, ostensibly for the last time. UNMIN's presence in Nepal was seen as having provided legitimacy to the Maoists by upholding the equivalency of the two armies. Conversely, the other major parties calculated that UNMIN's departure would make the Maoists more willing to compromise. UNMIN's poor management of the former rebels and their arsenal already had peeved India. Now it was angered by reports that UN officials were in touch with some Terai-based armed groups and had crossed over to the Indian side to interact with them to find evidence about their linkages with India. China saw the risk of the UNMIN process straying into extraneous areas that conflicted with its definition of peace.

Delay and Departure

After the constituent assembly failed to meet its May 28 deadline, the major parties agreed to a yearlong extension. Uncertainty persisted over the body's ability to deliver a new Constitution by the new deadline of April 13, 2011. There was a lack of consensus on several key issues, including whether to adopt a parliamentary or presidential executive system and what federalism model should be implemented. Federalism was a contentious issue. Many marginalised groups, including indigenous nationalities and Madhesis, wanted to restructure the state based on ethnic or regional identities, a plan the Maoists supported.

In 2007 and 2008, the interim government signed agreements with indigenous nationalities and Madhesis promising to fulfil this demand. However, there were conflicting claims to territory based on identity, most notably between the Tharus (an indigenous nationalities group from the Terai) and the Madhesis. The Nepali Congress opposed that form of federalism as did dominant groups such as high-caste Hindus. A state restructuring committee was working to resolve these issues. However, any efforts to implement federalism were likely to result in vehement protests irrespective of the mode selected.

With the 2008 elections, UNMIN's responsibility had been restricted to monitoring the two armies. Having to stand by helplessly during the intractability of subsequent phases of the peace process was becoming a source of considerable concern within the UN. On the other hand, the mainstream parties, Nepal Army and India began viewing UNMIN's public statements as being biased in favour of the Maoists. During its four-year tenure, contradictory interpretations of UNMIN's role proved highly controversial. It was a country-specific special political mission to provide a forward platform to help prevent and resolve conflict and support complex political transitions, in coordination with national actors and UN development and humanitarian entities on the ground. Headed by a special representative of the UN Secretary-General, it lacked the broad mandate traditional peace operations carried.

Still, UNMIN saw through the election to the 2008 constituent assembly, and even though the Maoist combatants were still in the cantonments by the time its mission ended, it preserved the peace between the two sides and laid the ground for the eventual disbandment of the Maoist army. (Thapa and Ramsbotham, 2017). UNMIN's tenure ended in January 2011, and the UCPN-Maoist handed over cantonments to the Army Integration Special Committee. The UN mission's departure brought new uncertainty to the peace process, heightened by the reality that Nepal remained under a caretaker government.

A secret seven-point pact between the UCPN-Maoist and Jhal Nath Khanal of the CPN-UML enabled him to win the 17th round of voting in February. However, it was soon revealed that Khanal had not consulted his own party before signing the private agreement with UCPN-Maoist chair Dahal. The opposition Nepali Congress and ruling party factions stepped up attacks on Khanal. One contentious aspect of the clandestine agreement was its proposal to create a separate armed force of Maoist ex-combatants or an alternative force that would combine the PLA with other security forces. Another was an arrangement between the CPN-UML and UCPN-Maoist to lead the government by turns. After prolonged deadlock, popular pressure grew for a national consensus government.

Khanal swore in his first cabinet members in March.

That month also underscored the growing relationship between the Chinese and Nepalese armies. General Chen Bingde, Chief of General Staff of the PLA, arrived in Kathmandu in the highest-level military visit from China to Nepal for over a decade. Chen met with the Nepalese prime minister and president, as well as with the chief of the Nepal Army. He announced a military assistance package worth $17 million from the PLA to the Nepal Army, with assurances of more support to come. Significantly, the military deals were signed not by the Chinese and Nepalese governments but by the respective military chiefs.

Chen's visit came in the aftermath of the Dalai Lama's decision to step down as the political leader of the Tibetan government-in-exile. The withdrawal of the Dalai Lama from a political role raised concerns of a rise in militancy among Tibetan exiles in India and Nepal, particularly among those who disagreed with his acceptance of Tibetan autonomy within China and pushed for full independence. Days after Chen's departure, Beijing recalled its ambassador, Qiu Guohong, before his three-year term expired, following purported rifts within the embassy over handling Tibetans in Nepal. This was Beijing's second successive ambassadorial recall from Kathmandu over the Tibet question (Upadhya, 2012)

Weeks later, the Chinese announced the appointment of Yang Houlan, the ambassador for Korean Peninsular Affairs, someone more senior in the Chinese diplomatic service and presumably with stronger credentials within the Chinese Communist Party. Educated in the United States, Yang had served as his country's ambassador to Afghanistan, another chronically unstable country on China's periphery. The appointment of a seasoned diplomat with such a clear and rich security affairs background was seen as stemming from Beijing's anxiety to ensure that Nepal's turmoil did not spill over into Tibet and beyond.

India remained by far the largest provider of military assistance to Nepal, pledging $55 million in 2009 alone. Yet the total assistance Chen pledged represented a substantial increase in China's military aid to Nepal. Beijing's desire to deal directly with the Nepal Army was thought to reflect Chinese confidence in its status to ensure stability. However, Indian sources were worried by a 'loyalty-trust' proposal put forth by Chen under which Nepal would deport Tibetan refugees to China to prevent the rise of a militant Tibetan émigré force. New Delhi noted that Beijing had made the proposal directly to the CPN-UML and UCPN-Maoists. There was no word on the Tibet deal from either side, which had come amid growing international criticism of Nepal on the Tibetan refugee issue. The Chinese also wanted to establish reciprocal rank between Chinese and Nepalese officers, akin to the relations between the Nepalese and Indian militaries. New Delhi purportedly thwarted this plan. In November, the Nepal Army chief paid a reciprocal visit to Beijing during which the two sides signed an agreement worth $7.7 million, mostly to modernise Nepal's military hospital.

Concerned by a fresh wave of antagonism unleashed by the Maoists against India, including a demand for a review of all hydropower projects, the Indian Embassy in Kathmandu began pressing the matter with Prime Minister Khanal. In April, External Affairs Minister SM Krishna arrived to convey a range of concerns, emphasise the importance of completing the peace process, and express India's commitment to help Nepal in its transition to a stable, inclusive, multiparty democracy. Dahal told the minister that the Maoists were not anti-Indian and instead wished to improve relations between Nepal and India "on a new basis". He also cautioned the minister about a rising 'interference' by India in Nepal's internal affairs. Opinion in India, too, was hardening against the wisdom of sidelining the Maoists, especially since it had contributed to a diminution of New Delhi's diplomatic dominance and allowed China to step in (Gupta, 2010).

In June, India signalled a shift in its approach by appointing Jayant Prasad as ambassador in Kathmandu, as the Nepal team in Delhi shed its hawkish elements. Prasad's predecessor, Rakesh Sood, had become one of the most controversial Indian ambassadors in Nepal, particularly for his staunch opposition to Maoist positions and 'brash mannerism'. Sood, who had assumed office on the eve of the Maoists' rise to power, was portrayed in the local media as openly interfering in Nepal's internal affairs. A UCPN-Maoist cadre had hurled shoes at the ambassador in Solukhumbu, near the Tibet border. Prasad, a career diplomat like Sood, was seen as calm and deliberative. His appointment was announced a week after Yang Houlan took over as Chinese ambassador.

The following month, Chinese media reported that the Asia Pacific Exchange and Cooperation (APEC) – a Hong-Kong-based foundation widely thought to have China's backing – had signed an agreement with the United Nations Industrial Development Organisation (UNIDO), to invest $3 billion in Lumbini. The project aimed to make a 'Mecca for

Buddhists', with train links, an international airport, hotels and a Buddhist university. However, the initiative also appeared to be strategically aimed at reducing the influence of the Dalai Lama and his followers by creating a focal point for Buddhism that was free from Tibetan influence.

The bizarre news caused an uproar in Nepal, where the government said it had never heard of the project. UNIDO officers refused to comment as they tried to discover how their organisation had been linked. The story took another curious turn when it was revealed that UCPN-Maoist leader Dahal and former crown prince Paras Shah were working together on the project. Shah was later removed after widespread negative comments. Dahal's next moves worried Indian intelligence agents already suspecting APEC to be a Chinese bridge between the Maoists and the monarchists. After presenting his party with a proposal to form a nationalist front, Dahal held a series of meetings with senior royalists (Sharma, 2019). The APEC project would be derailed by its contradictions.

Khanal, facing constant protest, reshuffled his cabinet a few more times before resigning on August 14. A 60-member Chinese delegation headed by President Hu Jintao's special envoy arrived on a scheduled visit for meetings with top politicians and ministers. The delegation, led by Zhou Yongkang, a senior member of the Standing Committee of the politburo of the CCP, included three ministers and four assistant ministers. The two sides signed a $50 million economic and technical cooperation, an agreement on providing a $24 million soft loan for a hydropower transmission line project, a $2.5 million security project meant to enhance the capacities of Nepal Police, and a preliminary agreement to provide other concessional loans.

Some analysts noted the eagerness of China to sign such major deals during a caretaker administration, particularly given any reservations the succeeding government might have. Zhou told senior CPN-UML leaders that despite some awkwardness, he had proceeded with the visit because Nepal was a country of the highest priority for China. Zhou put forward a five-point proposal to enhance ties between the two countries, which included: more high-level exchange visits; Chinese investment in a variety of sectors, including business, infrastructure, tourism and water resources; Chinese support for security in Nepal; people-to-people contacts and cultural exchanges; cooperation between political parties; and joint efforts to tackle food insecurity, climate change and the global economic recession.

No senior Indian official had arrived since External Affairs Minister Krishna in April. Finance Minister Pranab Mukherjee had put off his visit at the last minute. Despite efforts, Khanal could not schedule a visit to New Delhi, suggesting a level of distrust. Some Indians considered Khanal as part of the 'China lobby' in Nepal, while others recalled that he had originally given Dahal the green signal to sack Gen. Katawal (Jha, 2014). Those Indians felt vindicated by the developments occurring during Khanal's tenure.

Amid the internal churning in the Maoists rank, India was still unprepared to accept Dahal's return as prime minister. Yet New Delhi realised that it could no longer try to keep the largest party in the legislature out of power without alienating the Nepalese people. While the Madhes parties were always relatively closer to the Maoists than to other political parties, especially on federalism, they were becoming increasingly fragmented to their own detriment. Getting them to power collectively despite their differences became imperative to advancing the common agenda of greater inclusion.

It was against this background that UCPN-Maoist central committee member Baburam Bhattarai, with United Democratic Madhesi Front (UMDF) support, defeated Nepali Congress candidate Ram Chandra Poudel in a CA vote in late August to become prime minister. The soft-spoken Bhattarai's election offered some hope of an end to the extended political impasse. In his first act as prime minister, he handed over keys to containers holding PLA weapons to the Army Integration Special Committee. Radical factions within the UCPN-Maoist and international Maoist groups strongly criticised him for betraying the revolution.

Bhattarai, believed to wield some political influence in New Delhi, was expected to draw a more productive Indian approach to the peace process. As he prepared to visit India in mid-October, his UCPN-Maoist and other major parties cautioned Bhattarai not to raise 'controversial issues' such as the 1950 Indo-Nepal Treaty of Peace and Friendship, the 1965 Arms Assistance Agreement and new extradition and mutual legal assistance treaties. Within those limitations, Bhattarai's agenda in New Delhi focused on trade and commerce, health, education, infrastructure development. It still provoked a backlash back home. In signing a Bilateral Investment Promotion and Protection Agreement (BIPPA), Bhattarai was criticised for attempts to mollify India at the cost of Nepalese interests.

The major parties signed an agreement in November to integrate 6,500 Maoist combatants into the Nepal Army and rehabilitate others. The accord stipulated the creation of a Special Directorate of the Nepal Army, which would draw 65 percent of its personnel from the existing Nepal Army and 35 percent from the ranks of Maoist combatants. UNMIN verification teams had originally identified 19,602 combatants at seven cantonment sites in 2007. But only 16,508 combatants could be located by the December 1, 2011 completion of the 'regrouping' process overseen by the AISC, as required by the November agreement. The discrepancy fuelled longstanding speculation that PLA numbers had been inflated for political and financial gain during the UNMIN-led verification process.

Such allegations – coupled with the fact that over 40 percent of the corps opted for integration rather than retirement or rehabilitation – raised questions about the feasibility of implementing the November agreement, which had set a quota of only 6,500 combatants for integration. The agreement also stipulated that the UCPN-Maoist would disband the 'paramilitary structure' of the YCL and return property seized during the armed conflict. Condemning the move, a hardline faction of the UCPN-Maoist led by Mohan Baidya and Ram Bahadur Thapa threatened further unrest if Bhattarai continued to make such 'mistakes'.

As the spectre of a Maoist split loomed, Chinese Premier Wen Jiabao stopped briefly in Kathmandu on January 13 on his way to the Middle East. Originally scheduled to arrive the previous month, Wen had cancelled the visit at the last moment for undisclosed reasons. Some reports suggested Wen had put off the visit after that Bhattarai announced it to the media in violation of a prior understanding. Beijing was anxious to keep the visit secret until Wen's arrival to forestall protests by

Kathmandu-based Tibetan exiles and their supporters. Deputy Prime Minister and Home Minister Bijay Gachhadar later visited Beijing to assuage its concerns.

Wen, the most senior Chinese official to visit Nepal since Premier Zhu Rongji in 2001, held talks with Bhattarai, President Yadav and other political leaders. The two sides signed eight agreements on infrastructure development. The Chinese delegation agreed to provide a one-time grant of $20 million for Nepal's peace process. There were assurances of an increase in Beijing's annual grant for the development of hydropower projects, airports, roads and other infrastructure. A joint statement described Wen's visit as having taken Nepal-China relations to a 'new height'. Nepal reiterated its 'one China' policy and Beijing reiterated its pledge not to interfere in Nepal's internal affairs.

Domestic pressure was building on Bhattarai. The Supreme Court had ruled that the constituent assembly could not be extended beyond six months unless a state of emergency was declared. The verdict had resulted in repeated short extensions. A fourth and ostensibly final six-month extension gave the body until the end of May 2012 to complete its duties. Successive protests demanding a swift end to the Constitution-writing process wearied the people. Traditionally dominant groups began protests in a backlash against the increasing assertiveness of those demanding ethnic-based federalism and affirmative action policies.

Citizenship provisions, always controversial, also emerged as a divisive issue when a government minister was discovered to be holding Nepalese and Indian passports, along with a Tibetan refugee card. Bhattarai's offer of a general amnesty for 'political crimes' committed during the civil conflict prompted criticism from human rights organisations and political opponents and heightened fears of impunity. As the economy stymied, Nepalese continued to migrate overseas for work and sent remittances accounting for an estimated quarter of gross domestic product. While tourism growth provided some relief, people faced power cuts of up to 12 hours a day. With the Supreme Court having effectively imposed May 27, 2012, as the deadline for the constituent assembly to either deliver a Constitution or dissolve itself, the political leadership was racing against time. Further pressure came from widespread public discontent with members enjoying state benefits with the repeated extensions.

In fairness, the political parties had reached major deals, including on setting up an 11-province model. They had also agreed to a popularly elected president and a parliament-elected prime minister to address the respective preferences of the Maoists and the mainstream parties. Yet political rivalries, especially over government leadership, resulted in the constituent assembly's dissolution on May 27. Equally responsible were competing efforts behind the scenes by India and China to influence the outcome of the federalism debate. New Delhi, which had been pressing for a single Madhes province in the Terai, had come around to the idea of two. New Delhi considered it the best way of boosting Madhesi — and its own — influence on Nepal's polity. With up to five provinces now being envisaged in the Terai, India no longer seemed keen on a partial Constitution that might be improved through amendments.

From the outset, the Chinese were opposed to ethnicity-based provinces along the border with Tibet, considering the impact that might have on Tibet's stability. Ethnic groups opposed a partial Constitution fearing a conspiracy to foil federalism altogether. Clear cracks emerged between the Maoists and Madhesis who insisted on an ethnic model and the Nepali Congress and CPN-UML which hardened their opposition. Beijing benefited from these divergences.

Bereft of options amid the relentless rancour, the Bhattarai government unilaterally scheduled new elections for November 22, claiming legitimacy to continue in power as a government elected by the dissolved CA. The Nepali Congress and the CPN-UML saw Bhattarai's government as illegitimate and demanded his immediate resignation before deciding on fresh elections. Complicating the political climate was the internal factionalism gripping all major parties. In the Nepali Congress, Sher Bahadur Deuba and Ram Chandra Poudel were locked in a bitter struggle for the premiership.

As a compromise, the Nepali Congress named its president Sushil Koirala as the prime ministerial candidate for a consensus government. The CPN-UML saw deep cleavages develop between its leadership and lawmakers belonging to different ethnic groups over the former's opposition to accommodating ethnic identity in the federal system. The UCPN-Maoist formally split in June with Mohan Baidya forming the CPN-Maoist with Chandra Prakash Gajurel and Ram Bahadur Thapa. That formalised a long-running divide. Baidya believed the Maoists were on the verge of capturing the state in 2005 (Lovell, 2019). When the 12-point understanding was being negotiated in New Delhi, Baidya and Gajurel were locked up in separate prisons in different Indian cities. India had released them after Koirala and Dahal signed the CPA. Since their return to Nepal, Baidya and Gajurel continued to voice scepticism about the party's decision to enter mainstream politics. Bhattarai had represented the rival party line advocating an alliance with the parliamentary parties against the monarchy.

The US State Department's decision in early September to formally remove the UCPN-Maoist from its list of global terrorist groups injected a new element to the discourse. Washington may have sensed a risk of Beijing attempting to reduce the influence of India and the United States. The US government may also have finally come around to realising that the Maoists were a permanent force in Nepal's electoral politics. The delisting of the UCPN-Maoist came against a flurry of other US activity, including the resumption of the Peace Corps after an eight-year gap and the appointment of a new ambassador. The confluence of decisions also indicated that Washington might be preparing to chart a course in Nepal that was independent of India's, building upon its six-decade history of bilateral cooperation.

Behind these debates, the continuing standoff weakened the Nepalese state. In the absence of a legislature, the government relied on presidential ordinances to authorise funding and adopt policies. With President Yadav, officially a ceremonial president, playing a more prominent role, the parties' past criticism of royal assertiveness came to be seen in a more lenient light.

To break the deadlock, Bhattarai went to Dahal with a proposal to name as prime minister Sushil Koirala, the president of the Nepali Congress – the largest group in the dissolved assembly. Dahal, anxious to see Bhattarai out of office, began discussions with Nepali Congress and CPN-UML. A former NC general secretary, President Yadav, too, preferred Koirala. As the three began drafting an understanding on a consensus government, the Bhattarai cabinet prepared the constitutional-amendment order needed to hold a second election to a constituent assembly in the absence of parliament.

However, Indian intelligence agents camped in Kathmandu had proposed a non-political advisory council. Grasping that Koirala was unacceptable to India, Bhattarai insisted on staying in office with the support of the army and New Delhi. To make his new stance publicly palatable, Bhattarai insisted the Nepali Congress to join the government before he resigned, which Koirala rejected (Sharma, 2019).

Process in Pieces

After nearly a year of political turmoil and constitutional uncertainty, on March 14, Nepal's four major political forces—the UCPN-Maoist, Nepali Congress, CPN-UML, and UMDF signed an 11-point deal to form an election government. Chief Justice Khil Raj Regmi was appointed chief executive and formed a cabinet comprising retired senior bureaucrats. As part of the deal, the four parties formed a High Level Political Committee (HLPC) to guide and facilitate the elected government. Amid differences among the political parties on the inclusiveness of the electoral rolls, the number of seats in the new constituent assembly, threshold of votes to secure representation from the proportional lists, the Regmi government scheduled the CA elections for November 19.

The electorate remained disillusioned by the parties' performance during the four years of the first constituent assembly. Because they refused to support identity-based federalism, the Nepali Congress and CPN-UML suffered desertions of leaders from the Madhesi people and other marginalised groups. Differences, mainly over senior leadership positions and policies, surfaced between Maoist ex-premiers Dahal and Bhattarai, who later quit his post as party vice-chairman. The parties in UMDF were the most fragmented and underwent several splits based on individual political rivalries.

New uncertainty loomed over the elections as a UCPN-Maoist-led alliance of over 30 fringe parties announced a boycott of the polls. This alliance demanded the resignation of the election government and the postponement of the CA polls to reach a broader agreement on constitutional issues through an all-party round table conference. After several unsuccessful rounds of talks, the HLPC won over two major constituents, the Madhesi Janadhikar Forum-Nepal (MJF-N), led by Upendra Yadav; and the Federal Socialist Party, led by Ashok Rai, a former CPN-UML leader. The HLPC addressed their key demands, restoring the CA ranks to 601 members from 491 and dropping the minimum threshold requirement of 1% of the total votes cast nationwide to qualify for a proportional allocation of seats. Over 140,000 police and military personnel were deployed for the election.

While the election manifestoes reflected the major political parties' differences over the modes of federalism as well as governance, the campaigns focused on pledges to address the local and immediate concerns. The CA elections, hailed as free and fair by most observers, saw a nationwide voter turnout of over 70 percent. The Nepali Congress and CPN-UML, positioned second and third in the first CA, rose to first and second place. Between them, the Nepali Congress and CPN-UML captured close to two-thirds of the CA seats and almost half the popular votes. In another shift, former royalists rose from irrelevance to winning close to 40 seats, more than tripling their presence in the first CA. By contrast, the UCPN-Maoist, the largest party in the first constituent assembly, saw its popular vote plummet to 15 percent from 30 percent. Madhesi parties collectively won fewer than 50 seats. Power was back in the hands of the two parties that had dominated Nepal's politics during the 1990s.

Twice As Hard

THE ELECTORAL SURGE for the Nepali Congress and the CPN-UML contained both opportunities and risks. Their joint implacability on federalism having thwarted the first constituent assembly, the two major mainstream parties had the mandate to refocus the debate towards reaching a viable and acceptable model. All stakeholders – internal and external – recognised that the new constituent assembly could deliver a Constitution and complete the transition to democracy only through cooperation among the full spectrum of parties represented in the chamber. They also knew that such a partnership depended on power-sharing arrangements acceptable to all.

Given their history of sustained – albeit rocky – collaboration, the Nepali Congress and the CPN-UML could drive the reconciliation process to its logical conclusion. The two parties had written Nepal's 1990 Constitution that replaced three decades of partyless palace-led rule. Although their subsequent bickering, corruption and abuse polarised

Nepalese politics, these two parties had banded together to marginalise the monarchy and mainstream the Maoists.

In the deeply divided political landscape, the partnership between the traditional parties could easily raise the suspicions of the UCPN-Maoist and other disgruntled parties in the new assembly. The Maoists had launched their 'people's war' in 1996 partly against the excesses of parliamentary democracy. At different points, they were even ready to work with the monarchy to counter the Nepali Congress and the CPN-UML. Madhesi groups were the other face of Nepal's new aspirations. But they, too, were filled with politicians who had once been with either of the two dominant parties or with the Maoists. The path of protest and confrontation was wide open with enough twists and turns to derail the peace process.

The next order of business forced upon the Nepalese, however, was a crude spectacle of institutional entanglement. A non-party caretaker administration of retired bureaucrats had been installed to conduct the elections because of the intense political squabbling. With the elections over, the normal political institutions and processes were poised to take over. Instead, President Ram Baran Yadav and chief executive Khil Raj Regmi clashed over who should call the inaugural session of the second constituent assembly.

Both sides reached for precedent – to little avail. Yadav urged Regmi to adhere to the universal parliamentary practice of the head of state performing that task. In response, Regmi cited the precedent of Prime Minister Girija Prasad Koirala summoning the first constituent assembly in 2008. But the cases were different and arose from exceptional circumstances. Prime Minister Koirala was acting head of state as well, as part of the deal key political parties had struck for the transition. Regmi, while heading the election government under extraordinary circumstances, continued to serve as chief justice concurrently.

Amid that tightening knot, in mid-January, Foreign and Home Minister Madhav Prasad Ghimire flew into New Delhi on an official visit. He held talks with Prime Minister Manmohan Singh and External Affairs Minister Salman Khurshid on political developments and progress on bilateral cooperation. If the constitutional tangle was discussed – as it must have been, given the Indian origins of this particular caretaker government model – it was done so privately.

China, for its part, was becoming more closely drawn into unification efforts of the UCPN-Maoist and its breakaway CPN-Maoist faction. Optimism had grown in both parties since October when visiting Chinese Vice Minister of International Department Ai Ping counselled such unity for the sake of bringing out the Constitution and ensuring political stability. But those imperatives only explained part of Beijing's interest.

Wary of the preponderance of India and the United States in Nepal, China considered a unified and powerful Maoist party conducive to its security concerns. Ai, visiting Nepal as a special envoy of the new President Xi Jinping, was considered China's point man on Nepal. Believed to enjoy close ties with Dahal, Ai focused his visit on meetings with top Maoist leaders from both factions. In recent interactions in Kathmandu and Beijing, according to one Nepalese interlocutor, the Chinese had consistently pressed – going beyond merely suggesting – the two Maoist factions to unite.

Yang Jiechi, now promoted from foreign minister to State Councillor, also had stressed the imperative of unification during his visit in July 2013. Considering the external and internal challenges Nepal's Maoists faced after their electoral defeat, one leading Chinese analyst contended, unification was the only way forward. Although immediate unity seemed unlikely, another Chinese expert suggested, the two factions could come together in time for the next general election – words that would prove to be more than prophetic. Careful to reiterate his country's usual caveat that this was an internal issue for Nepal, a Chinese Communist Party source confirmed that Nepalese Maoists from both factions were in regular touch with counterparts in Beijing.

Stronger relations with Nepal would not only help Beijing maintain better control in Tibet, the thinking went, they would also provide China with an opportunity to check Indian influence in the region. Amid a spurt in high-level political and military exchanges, China's direct investment in Nepal had nearly doubled between 2007 and 2011. Beijing continued to expand its involvement such diverse sectors as the military, roads, telecommunications, infrastructure, food supplies and hydroelectric power. Culture and language, while a new arena of cooperation, had expanded to the point where 70 schools in Nepal now offered courses in Mandarin, mostly through Chinese instructors.

Beijing was also helping Nepal develop Lord Buddha's birthplace as an international destination. In 1967, then UN Secretary-General U Thant had visited Lumbini and called for its preservation as a world pilgrimage site. In recent years, despite the fiasco involving a UN agency and pro-Chinese nongovernment organisation, Beijing had begun supporting an elaborate development plan for Lumbini that could eventually connect the pilgrimage with China via train.

The north-central region of Mustang was once again drawing Beijing's particular interest. In the 1960s, US Central Intelligence Agency-backed pro-independence Tibetan Khampa fighters used the area to mount an insurgency against Chinese communist rule. China was now building a road in the area it considered strategically crucial to its effort to engage with Nepal, control the flight of Tibetans, and revive ancient trade routes. Responding to Beijing's repeated concerns over the presence of foreign security personnel in the region, Kathmandu had tightened monitoring and surveillance. All this exacerbated India's worries that growing Chinese influence would increase its own vulnerabilities in Nepal.

IN FEBRUARY SUSHIL KOIRALA, the 74-year-old president of the Nepali Congress, was sworn in as prime minister, leading a coalition primarily backed by the CPN-UML. A member of the powerful clan dominating the party, Sushil was cousin to three prime ministers. A bachelor widely respected for his austere lifestyle, Sushil was not known as a dynamic leader and lacked executive experience. It was uncertain how effectively he could implement policies addressing Nepal's deepening inefficiencies. The Rastriya Prajatantra Party-Nepal (RPP-N), with the fourth-largest number of seats in the legislature, wanted Nepal to declare itself a Hindu state once again. The only party openly advocating the monarchy after the king stepped down, the RPP-N appeared to have muted its position on the crown.

Nepal continued to be governed under the interim

Constitution of 2007, with profound disagreements persisting on the contents of its successor. While most parties agreed to a federal model, the Maoists and their allies continued to advocate districts based on ethnic identity. The Nepali Congress and CPN-UML preferred a non-ethnic administrative model, perhaps with even greater zeal, now that they even felt vindicated in the polls.

In his first public speech on foreign policy, Prime Minister Koirala described China and India as the top priorities of his government. In a briefing to the diplomatic community in Kathmandu, Koirala also said his government would not tolerate activities from Nepalese soil against neighbours. That pledge came as the Foreign Ministry rejected a report by US-based Human Rights Watch that Tibetan refugees in Nepal were facing greater restrictions under Chinese pressure. The ministry described such reports as 'unnecessary meddling' in Nepal-China relations.

As India and China both expressed concern that creating or reorganising districts could lead to instability along their respective borders, Nepal worked to balance ties with both neighbours. Koirala visited China in June 2014 to attend the South Asia Expo, during which Beijing pledged continued financial and infrastructure support to Nepal. Chinese inroads under the Maoist-led government had caused much anxiety in India, prompting major overtures to enhance its own ties with Nepal.

The visit of India's new Prime Minister Narendra Modi in August provided a significant opportunity to reset the relationship. The first Indian premier on a bilateral visit to Nepal since 1997, Modi committed US$1 billion in aid and loans. Given the Nepali Congress's historically close ties to India, its return to power was considered a good augury. Public enthusiasm and positive media coverage helped the government's determination to make the visit a success.

Addressing parliament in Hindi, Modi sought to dispel many traditional Nepalese misgivings about Indian policy. He made an explicit declaration of non-interference in the internal affairs of Nepal. Modi's firm affirmation of India's support to democracy and development in Nepal was also aimed to quell rumours that the Bharatiya Janata Party (BJP)'s Hindu nationalist government wanted to restore the monarchy and/ or Hindu statehood. Although the Hindu elements had taken a back seat to 'progress' and 'economic development' in Modi's campaign, many Nepalese saw the BJP and Modi personally as firm champions of Hindu values. During his frequent visits to India on personal and religious engagements, former king Gyanendra continued meeting with senior Congress and BJP leaders, deepening Nepalese suspicions of India's motives.

There were reports that Modi – who as chief minister of the Gujarat state had met Gyanendra both as king and commoner – was keen on meeting the ex-monarch during his visit but was advised against that. Since the April 2006 transfer of power, India and the rest of the world had publicly shunned him on Nepalese soil. Recognising that the BJP could not promote the Hindu agenda in Nepal for fear of being seen as interfering, Nepalese were aware of the other channels the Modi government could mobilise, including nongovernmental, fraternal and religious organisations. In an effort to assuage longstanding Nepalese concerns, Modi also reiterated his government's willingness to revise the 1950 Peace and Friendship Treaty in keeping with the times and sought Nepal's specific inputs.

Chinese wariness of India's intentions in Nepal had grown since Modi's election earlier in the year. Thus, Beijing appeared satisfied with the lack of progress on an India-Nepal power trade agreement, although Kathmandu and New Delhi would sign it two months later. Chinese analysts insisted that Beijing would oppose any attempt by the new Indian government to use Nepal for its strategic interests. One reason for Beijing's growing suspicions appeared to stem from Modi's delay in responding to an invitation to visit China, although he had swiftly agreed to visit the United States and Japan. The China-friendly attitude Modi had exhibited as chief minister of Gujarat seemed to have waned with his election as prime minister, one Chinese analyst suggested.

Amid these geostrategic undercurrents, Nepal turned its attention to regional diplomacy. It hosted the long-delayed South Asian Association for Regional Cooperation (SAARC) Summit in Kathmandu in late November, the first such high-level gathering in three years. Modi had created momentum for a summit by inviting the heads of all SAARC nations to his inauguration. There were bilateral attributes to Modi's second visit to Kathmandu in three months, as he inaugurated Indian-aided projects.

A key development during the 18th SAARC summit was China's push to elevate its role in the organisation from an observer to that of an active member. However, Nepal put that off by insisting it needed to consult with other member states first. A symbolic achievement for Nepal, the summit produced little of substance. Of the three connectivity agreements considered, only one on electricity was signed. There was no substantial progress on a South Asia Free Trade Agreement and SAARC Agreement on Trade in Services.

As Nepalese renewed their focus on a new Constitution with the advent of 2015, former prime minister and senior CPN-UML leader Jhal Nath Khanal expressed happiness at the 'neutral position' Beijing had exhibited during the drafting process. Khanal's praise of China carried more than subtle hints of his party's view that western countries and India were backing the UCPN-Maoist-led opposition alliance.

In late March, as Maoist leader Dahal left on a visit to Beijing for talks with Chinese Communist Party officials, President Ram Baran Yadav attended the Boao Forum Asia in Hainan province. Meeting with Yadav on the summit sidelines, President Xi urged the two countries to strengthen cooperation in interconnectivity, infrastructure, and hydropower development. He expressed China's willingness to begin talks on a free trade agreement with Nepal at the earliest. Earlier that month, China had increased its annual aid to Nepal to $128 million from $24 million.

Xi expressed Chinese appreciation for Nepal's firm support on issues concerning China's core interests, including Tibet and Taiwan, and pledged to support Nepal's efforts to safeguard its independence, sovereignty and territorial integrity. Xi also invited Nepal to take part in China's new One Belt One Road (OBOR) initiative. Yadav reiterated Nepal's longstanding pledge that it would never allow its soil to be used for anti-China activities.

For India, these developments made Nepal overdue for an updated assessment. Foreign Secretary S. Jaishankar arrived on a two-day visit in early April to take stock of Nepal's political situation and seek backing for New Delhi's candidacy for a seat on the UN Security Council. Nepal also appointed a new ambassador to India, filling a post lying vacant for three and a half years since the Maoists recalled the incumbent. Although Deep Kumar Upadhyaya, a leading member of the Nepali Congress, lacked diplomatic experience, he was thought to enjoy good relations with Indian leaders across the political spectrum.

In a major decision, Nepal's investment board cleared China's Three Gorges International Corp to build a $1.6 billion 750-megawatt hydropower project, the largest Chinese investment in Nepal. The hydropower projects built in the last few decades were smaller run-of-the-river types, where power generation peaked during the monsoon underperformed and ebbed in the dry season. Nepal's hydropower sector had been a preserve of Indian investment for long, a tradition the latest deal sought to break. At a time when mega reservoir-type projects faced tough resistance from local activists and communities whose lands would be submerged, Kathmandu needed to factor in New Delhi's reaction. Shortly thereafter Koirala left for talks in Jakarta with President Xi on the sidelines of the Asian-African Summit, where he also met Indian Foreign Minister Sushma Swaraj.

Quake Cooperation

Sino-Indian rivalry sharply swerved into the arena of humanitarian relief as a powerful wave of earthquakes shook Nepal in the final week of April. The first earthquake, registering magnitude 7.8 on the Richter scale, occurred shortly before noon on April 25, with an epicentre in the central-Nepalese district of Gorkha. Over 8,000 people were reported killed by the quake and ensuing avalanche, and over half a million homes were damaged or destroyed. After two weeks of relentless aftershocks, a 7.3-magnitude earthquake struck the same fault-line again, followed minutes later by a 6.3-magnitude one. Several structures damaged in the first tremor toppled during subsequent ones.

As average Nepalese spontaneously reached out to help, the international community offered generous aid. At the forefront were Nepal's neighbours. Under Operation Friendship, India deployed 13 aircraft and over 500 rescuers and provided water, food, equipment and medical supplies. China sent 62 rescuers plus blankets, tents and generators and announced plans to send four planes and an additional 170 soldiers. Pakistan sent four cargo planes full of supplies, including concrete cutters and sniffer dogs.

Foreign Secretary Jaishankar and National Security Adviser Ajit Doval landed in Nepal to review the relief and rescue efforts. New Delhi saw the relief operations as statements of capability as much as responsibility (Jaishankar 2020). Some leading Nepalese opposition figures complained of India's lack of sensitivity for the country's sovereignty during the relief work. Nepalese media reported that Indian intelligence agents posing as reporters and relief workers had travelled close to the Chinese border, prompting pushback from Beijing. Indian media coverage was criticised for being shrill, jingoistic and, in some cases, outright erroneous. China was not spared, either.

As Beijing pledged a new round of assistance based on Nepal's needs and China's relief experience, its contingent of over 500 People's Armed Police came in for criticism for initially refusing to coordinate with other militaries, violating international best practices and potentially contributing to avoidable loss of life.

Undaunted, China and India pressed on with the 'disaster diplomacy'. At a donors' conference in Kathmandu in June, Chinese Foreign Minister Wang Yi said his country would enhance coordination with India in reconstruction. During Prime Minister Modi's visit to Beijing in May, Wang recalled, Chinese leaders had proposed a trilateral economic corridor, which elicited a positive response from Modi. Indian Foreign Minister Swaraj expressed readiness to advance trilateral cooperation through a joint working group. The international community pledged Nepal $4 billion for reconstruction, with India alone committing $1 billion.

The prospects for Sino-Indian amity on Nepal were overshadowed by the report that the two Asian giants had agreed to use a trade route in disputed territory in far western Nepal near the tri-country border. Maoist leader Dahal sent protest letters to Modi and Xi, urging them to rectify the May 25 pact on Lipulekh. Dahal said the agreement violated the 1816 Sugauli Treaty between Nepal and British India, under which Lipulekh belonged to Nepal. In New Delhi, ambassador Deep Upadhyaya said the issue had been taken up at the highest levels. Kalapani, of which Lipulekh was a part, and Susta were the two disputed territories still on the agenda of foreign secretary-level talks between Nepal and India. Upadhyaya urged New Delhi and Beijing to address Nepal's genuine concerns by taking the necessary steps to correct the agreement.

Dahal and Nepali Congress leader Sher Bahadur Deuba visited New Delhi for talks with Modi and other Indian leaders on ways of ensuring broader consensus to promulgate the new

Constitution. While it was unclear whether either leader raised Lipulekh with Modi or other Indian interlocutors, Deuba did so in an address to a leading New Delhi think tank.

Impelled by the earthquake-induced urgency across the political spectrum, the ruling coalition and the opposition UCPN-M signed a 16-point deal in early June to fast-track the Constitution, saying it would enable a more effective earthquake response. The government completed a draft Constitution the following month and subsequently released it for public hearings. Protests against the arbitrary imposition of the Constitution, which had begun after the 16-point agreement, now grew across the country. The Nepal Sadbhavana Party, with six members, quit the constituent assembly. Amid the escalating violence, Indian ambassador Ranjit Rae rejected Deputy Prime Minister Bam Dev Gautam's claim that many intruders from India had fanned the protests.

In response to a petition challenging the constitutionality of the 16-point agreement, the Supreme Court ruled that the constituent assembly was required to delineate state boundaries as part of the new Constitution. In early August, the four parties issued a map with proposed state boundaries without formal consultation with Madhesi, Tharu, janajati or Dalit groups. Moreover, the parties did not explain why they had discarded their earlier formula of eight states. Madhesi, Tharu and janajati groups said the proposed divisions violated principles that had either been agreed in previous deals or were still being worked out. Clashes in western Nepal's Kailali district between security forces and protesters demanding a separate province for Tharus killed 20 people, including 17 police officers, and injured 100. In a telephone call to Koirala to express sorrow,

Modi also voiced India's concern that such instability would compound the tragedy caused by the earthquake.

The constituent assembly adopted the constitution bill by a lopsided 507-25 vote on September 17 and sent it to President Yadav for promulgation. Of the 598 assembly members, 532 cast their votes: 25 members of the monarchist pro-Hindu RPP-N voted against, whereas 66 other members abstained. They included members of Madhesi, Tharu, and pro-federalism parties, two from the Nepali Congress, one from the UCPN-M and one independent. In defining the majority Hindu nation as a secular republic divided into seven federal provinces, the new Constitution broadly conformed to the three-pronged agenda for change advanced by the major parties. Persisting beneath the surface was the conflict between those seeking to maintain the status quo to protect the country and those fighting against it to end discrimination and marginalisation.

Predictably, widespread relief was accompanied by serious discontent. Several regional parties, mainly in the Terai, rejected the Constitution and its formula of seven states. Regional leaders insisted that lawmakers in Kathmandu had drawn borders to keep ethnic groups weak and divided. Upendra Yadav, chairman of Federal Socialist Forum Nepal, the biggest party in the Madhes leading the protests, wanted the 22 districts in the region partitioned into one or two states. Raj Kumar Lekhi, a leader of the over 1.7 million-strong Tharu community – the fourth largest ethnic community in Nepal – also rejected the Constitution. He said two provinces in Madhes – one for Tharu and another for the Madhesi – would satisfy both groups. Others worried that assigning specific provinces to specific ethnic or social groups risked fragmenting the country.

New Delhi, which had set the process in motion a decade earlier, did not consider the new Constitution broad-based enough. In August and September, 45 people were killed in clashes with police. India was concerned that continued grievances could escalate into violence that could spill over into its territory. Before President Yadav officially ratified the basic law, Modi sent his top diplomat to convey New Delhi's concerns. Foreign Secretary S. Jaishankar held talks with Yadav, Koirala and leaders of all the major political parties, including those opposing the Constitution. The Indian envoy wanted Nepal to delay the Constitution for more discussions with disgruntled groups. Sensitive to the domestic stakes involved, leaders of the major parties almost universally expressed their inability to do so at such late stage. Koirala, Dahal and Oli – the heads of the three major parties – were said to have been the most vocal.

Despite private reservations, President Yadav was bound by his ceremonial role. Hours before the ratification ceremony on September 20, ambassador Ranjit Rae spoke to Prime Minister Koirala to express Delhi's disappointment that the process was going through. He then flew to New Delhi for consultations. The External Affairs Ministry issued a terse statement merely 'noting' the promulgation of the new Constitution. It expressed India's concern that the situation in several parts of the country bordering India continued to be violent. New Delhi reiterated its call that issues on which there were differences should be resolved through dialogue in an atmosphere free from violence and intimidation, and institutionalised to enable broad-based ownership and acceptance. China offered a far more ringing endorsement. "As a friendly neighbour, the Chinese side notes with pleasure that Nepal's constituent assembly has endorsed the new constitution," its Foreign Ministry spokesperson said in Beijing.

India's concern with the violent reaction to the Constitution in the Terai arose from the 1,751 km open border it shared with Nepal. As local people travelled freely, the ease with which smugglers, human traffickers and terror suspects also moved concerned Indian security agencies. Communities living in the Terai, especially the Madhesis and the Tharu ethnic minorities – making up nearly 40 percent of Nepal's population – expressed concern that the proposed boundaries of the new provinces could lead to their political marginalisation. Madhesis shared close ethnic ties with people in India. India believed it had received assurances from Nepalese leaders that those concerns would be addressed.

India's concern also stemmed from the way the Constitution was rushed through. Important procedures were shortened to irrelevance, as with the public consultation phase, or discarded. Many members complained they were not given enough time to read the nearly 150-page draft (ICG, 2016). Some saw a small band of leaders guided by their own political reasons: Koirala to vacate the premiership in favour of Oli to become president of Nepal, Deuba to take over as Nepali Congress president, and Dahal to regain influence amid deepening Maoist divisions. Standing up to India to adopt a much-delayed Constitution bolstered the political class's diminishing nationalist credentials.

Another significant source of concern for New Delhi was the perception that Beijing had blindsided it. Foreign Minister Wang Yi, Vice Minister Chen Fengxian and Assistant Minister

Dou Enyong all visited Nepal in August as the constituent assembly debated the draft. Some Indian sources believed China had persuaded Dahal and the Maoists to drop their fierce opposition to the draft suddenly. Other Indians, including those who had played leading roles in 2006, cautioned against overreaction. They felt the concerns of the Madhesis could be addressed through future amendments as Nepal's Constitution matured and evolved.

The United Nations, too, had initially issued a rather terse statement attributed to Secretary-General Ban Ki-moon that merely 'acknowledged' the adoption of the Constitution. Despite decades of development partnerships and support for the peace process, the international community muted its reaction to the protests. Western donors had been facing mounting criticism that they promoted culturally inappropriate liberal values and muddied the waters in the first CA. Amid new pressures to channel development funds through the government and to show results via spending, they were less likely to be outspoken (ICG 2016). Still, the lukewarm reaction from the organisation that had played an essential role in the country's peace process surprised and even dismayed many Nepalese. Four days later, the UN issued a second statement in which Ban commended the Nepalese people on the adoption of the new Constitution. In both statements, the UN Secretary-General emphasised the importance of non-violence and respect for peaceful protests.

In a surprise move, former premier Baburam Bhattarai announced his resignation from the UCPN-Maoist as well as parliament and expressed support for the Madhesi demands. Claiming that India had imposed an unannounced blockade on Nepal, the former premier also asked the government to take diplomatic initiatives to solve the issue at the earliest. Bhattarai, who headed a key CA panel formed to forge a consensus on contentious issues, had skipped the official celebrations suggesting that half the country was in bereavement. Still, speculation swirled that Bhattarai, known to be close to India, might have received 'signals' from New Delhi. Those claims were fuelled by Indian media commentaries suggesting that Bhattarai's departure provided New Delhi with an opportunity to ensure its suggestions on the Constitution were accommodated.

Leading Kathmandu-based politicians and commentators already had been arguing that India fomented the agitation in the Madhes. The perception was growing in the country that the Madhesi community figured in India's policy calculus much like the Sri Lankan Tamils once did. The discord thus stemmed from India's demand that the Madhesis made up about a third of the Nepalese population – in no small measure due to massive migration from the Indian hinterland – must have constitutionally mandated full citizenship rights and proportional representation in the government and security forces. The Nepalese contrasted that demand with the status of India's Muslims who, despite constituting over 15 percent of a 1.35 billion population enjoyed infinitesimal representation in their country's institutions. From the perspective of a sizeable number of Nepalese, if Madhesis dominated national politics amid disunity and fragmentation of other groups, India could expect to retain a powerful voice.

An Indian newspaper report just days after the blockade described in detail the amendments India had sought. The changes sought included shifting to full proportional representation in parliament and other political bodies. Many of India's other suggestions focused on controversial clauses that hurt the Madhesi. They included citizenship restrictions for people born in Nepal of foreign fathers, many of whom were Indian, and restrictions, based on definitions of Nepalese descent, on who was eligible for leadership positions such as the prime minister, president and vice president.

Ambassador Ranjit Rae denied New Delhi had made those recommendations. Other Indian sources said the published list of proposed amendments were compiled by Madhesis and sent to New Delhi, which a scoop-hungry reporter presented as official. Still, the content and the timing of the media report was enough for many Nepalese to see the blockade as another Indian assault on their national sovereignty. Some seasoned Nepal hands in India, including former ambassadors in Kathmandu, could be heard lamenting how the same leaders who once sought – and received – strong Indian support for Nepal's democratic struggle were now the first to decry Indian interference. Others saw the current crisis as an outcome of India's readiness to entertain Nepalese leaders who would tell people in New Delhi what they wanted to hear, while going back home to do what they wanted to do.

The major Nepalese parties, for their part, moved to the next item of the 16-point agreement: electing a new prime minister and president. Khadga Prasad Sharma Oli, chief of the CPN-UML, was sworn in as prime minister on October 12, after he defeated incumbent Sushil Koirala 338-249 in the parliamentary contest. In the 1990s, Oli carried a reputation as an India-friendly leader in a party that traditionally viewed New Delhi with much suspicion. He was instrumental in parliament's endorsement of the Mahakali Treaty, a decision that went on to split the CPN-UML. Privately sceptical of the course charted by the 2005 12-point understanding in New Delhi, Oli had become a fierce critic of the Maoists. In recent years, he was among the strongest opponents of the federalism model proposed by Madhesi and indigenous groups.

In a palpable gesture to disgruntled groups, he appointed two deputies from parties that opposed different elements of the Constitution: Kamal Thapa, head of the royalist Rastriya Prajatantra Party Nepal (RPP-N) and Bijay Kumar Gachhadar who led one of the Madhesi parties. Nepal's Maoists, too, served alongside the royalists in the cabinet for the first time. The Nepali Congress, despite being the largest party in parliament, sat in the opposition.

The following week, the constituent assembly unanimously elected UCPN-Maoist leader Onsari Gharti Magar as Nepal's first woman speaker of parliament. History was still to be made. On October 28, parliament elected CPN-UML lawmaker Bidya Bhandari as Nepal's first woman president and second head of state after it became a republic. She defeated her opponent from the Nepali Congress Kul Bahadur Gurung by 327 to 214 votes to replace Ram Baran Yadav, whose original two-year tenure was extended with the prolonged constitution-writing process.

Bhandari, who joined politics in her teens, rose to prominence after her husband – CPN-UML general secretary Madan Bhandari – died in a vehicle accident in 1993. Riding a wave of sympathy, she defeated former prime minister Krishna Prasad Bhattarai of the Nepali Congress in a by-election for her late husband's parliamentary seat the following year.

Campaigners hailed Bhandari, who served as defence minister from 2009 to 2011, for her firm stance in favour of increasing female representation in parliament to 33 percent. Although she gave up her party membership after becoming president, Bhandari belonged to the Oli faction in the NCP. Cordial working relations between the new president and prime minister was a good portent. Still, the Nepalese people now waded deeper into uncharted waters, with each of its giant neighbours bracing for the unknown.

New Constitution,
New Contentions

IF THE ADOPTION of a new Constitution embittered Nepal's relations with India, it allowed China to accelerate long-term engagement in more areas. As public unrest escalated in the Terai, the Nepalese began feeling the harsher effects of the informal Indian border blockade. Extra measures in place on the Indian side allowed people to continue crossing the border freely but restricted movement of crucial Indian and third-country goods into Nepal. This mostly occurred through stricter inspection of trucks and a sudden spurt in the 'discovery' of violations. In Kathmandu, prices of petroleum and cooking gas skyrocketed as black markets proliferated.

In October 2015, Deputy Prime Minister and Foreign Minister Kamal Thapa returned from talks in New Delhi with what he considered were positive assurances. Yet the blockade continued, as did economic hardships across the country. As Thapa's public comments turned rancorous, the bilateral acrimony shifted to the United Nations. Presenting Nepal's report at the UN Human Rights Council in Geneva, Thapa said the border blockade had curtailed Nepal's rights as a land-locked country. His comments came after a statement from the US Embassy in Kathmandu warning of a looming humanitarian crisis. India's representative raised the issue of war crimes committed during Nepal's decade-long conflict, marking the first time New Delhi had done so in an international forum. Considering that New Delhi had shielded Kathmandu from international opprobrium at a similar session during the royal regime, India's move signalled a sharp escalation in the bilateral dispute. Predictably, the Indian representative's intervention prompted a sharp rebuke not only from Thapa but also from Premier Oli in Kathmandu.

The bitterness intensified later in the month after Prime Minister Modi and his British counterpart David Cameron held talks in London partly covering Nepal. A joint statement stressed the importance of a lasting and inclusive constitutional settlement in Nepal that would address the remaining areas of concern and promote political stability and economic growth. Now sensing a New Delhi-led campaign against the Constitution, Kathmandu stepped up accusations of foreign interference. Nepal insisted that it had adopted the new Constitution as a sovereign country and would not allow other countries to dictate its content. Protesters in various parts in Nepal burned effigies of Modi, as Nepalese media distributors boycotted Indian television and movies. The border blockade escalated to the point where Nepal requested its first-ever fuel shipments from China.

Thapa flew to Beijing in December, where the two countries signed a long-term agreement aimed at ending India's monopoly on Nepal's fuel imports. Addressing a joint news conference, Foreign Minister Wang Yi said Nepal should not become a 'boxing arena' between India and China. Reacting to India's indirect support to the Madhesi movement – without referring to the protests – Wang said China and Nepal had always treated each other sincerely and as equals and hoped India would adopt the same policy and practices.

Pressure mounted on the Modi government from Indian opposition parties as well, which insisted that China took advantage of a series of Indian missteps in Nepal. In attacking the government, leaders of the main opposition Congress party brushed aside the role of their government's official embargo 26 years earlier in alienating the Nepalese psyche. Government policy makers continued to insist that Nepalese leaders not only ignored New Delhi's pleas for an inclusive Constitution but also refused to honour promises of greater consultations they had made to the Madhesi and janjati communities.

Modi government sources did not think any effort Nepal made to mobilise China against the closures would be practical in the long term. They also believed pressure from the United States, Japan and the European Union would lead Kathmandu to reach an accommodation with the marginalised groups eventually. Amid this political divide in New Delhi, sections of India's strategic community contended that punishing an entire population to pressure the ruling elite was inherently counter-productive. Even if Nepal could not effectively mobilise the 'China card' right away, the lingering unpleasantness created by the situation would create opportunities for Beijing that could ultimately prove disastrous for New Delhi.

Yet reconciliation efforts continued at other levels. Early

in the new year, Nepal and India formed an Eminent Persons Group to review all bilateral agreements and treaties, including the controversial 1950 Treaty of Peace and Friendship. Comprising relevant experts from India and Nepal, the Indian side was led by parliamentarian Bhagat Singh Koshyari, a senior leader of the ruling BJP, and the Nepalese side by Bhekh Bahadur Thapa, a former foreign affairs and finance minister. The Nepalese prime minister had vowed not to visit India until it lifted the blockade, at one point, even threatening to visit China first. By February 2016, distraught Nepalese citizens forced Madhesi protesters back from the Raxaul–Birgunj border crossing, the only one of six key passages blocked on the Nepal side. Shortly after that, Madhesi protesters relented, and the informal Indian blockade of other crossings ended.

With the stage having been set for an understanding, Oli visited New Delhi later in February disavowing any 'China card' against India. Even in the midst of such rhetorical flourishes, the Oli government recognised the significance of maintaining all channels of communication with India. Oli held talks with Modi, and other key Indian leaders, and the two countries signed seven agreements spanning areas such as Nepal's post-earthquake reconstruction and enhancing connectivity and transit facilities. Oli described the visit as having normalised bilateral relations, but there were still enough signs of strains. The two sides failed to issue a joint statement. Although no official reason was given, Nepal was not happy about India's refusal to commend the Constitution unconditionally. While Modi described the new Constitution as a major achievement, he also reiterated the need for greater efforts to accommodate all aspirations.

Three weeks later, Oli travelled to China, where the two countries signed 10 agreements, including a landmark deal on transit trade aimed at reducing Nepal's overwhelming economic dependence on India. The transit agreement gave the landlocked Himalayan country access to the sea via the Chinese ports of Tianjin, Shenzhen, Lianyungang and Zhanjiang. Nepal could also use dry docks at Lanzhou, Lhasa and Xigatse for third-country trade. Besides, Nepal became a dialogue partner of the Shanghai Cooperation Organization.

Oli also signed a memorandum of understanding on building railways from China to Nepal. The provision for connecting the railways to Lumbini, near the border with India, drew New Delhi's firm disapproval and was later changed to ending tracks up to Kathmandu. General opinion on the visit was mixed in Nepal and India. With Tianjin situated 3,000 km away from Nepal – three times the distance to India's Haldia – expectations of an immediate benefit were low. India also had offered Nepal use of its Visakhapatnam port, already connected by viable transport infrastructure. Rail routes to key Chinese manufacturing hubs had the potential to boost the volume of Nepal's trade with and through China. However, the Himalayas' treacherous terrain and hostile weather were expected to pose severe costs.

Acknowledging that geographic, political, economic, historical and religious factors allowed India to exert greater influence on Nepal, Chinese official media probed new possibilities. Still, Nepal could assume the role of a valuable bridge between China and India, if New Delhi changed its "a zero-sum mentality", an attribute Beijing saw becoming more pronounced with the Modi government. On a more ominous note, the Global Times said: "China's Nepal policy could take the interests of Nepalese ethnic groups of Indian origin into account, but China won't meddle in Nepal's domestic political disputes." That comment came after Madhesi leaders expressed dissatisfaction with China's support for the new Constitution. Rajendra Mahato criticised Beijing for "hurting the sentiment of one-third of Nepali people". Madhesi and janajati leaders had met ambassador Wu Chuntai and urged Beijing to mount diplomatic pressure on Kathmandu to amend the new Constitution.

In April, a European Union-India joint statement containing a reference to Nepal's Constitution returned to dog relations with India. Part of the statement stated that "India and the EU have agreed on the need for a lasting and inclusive constitutional settlement in Nepal that will address the remaining constitutional issues in a time-bound manner, and promote political stability and economic growth." The Nepalese Ministry of Foreign Affairs fired back: "The EU-India joint statement not only hurts the sentiments of the people of Nepal but also defies the fundamental principle of non-interference in internal affairs of a country in breach of UN Charter and norms of international law." Other Nepalese, however, considered the statement innocuous enough, especially since many legislators who had voted for the Constitution now also sought amendments.

The onset of a new chill in relations was further underscored in early May when Nepal recalled its ambassador Deep Upadhyaya for allegedly working against the national interest. That announcement came after President Bidya Bhandari called off her first visit to India as head of state, citing domestic preoccupations. Soon, Oli loyalists began accusing Upadhyaya of involvement in a plot to topple the government, exceeding his brief, and accompanying Indian ambassador Ranjit Rae on a visit to western Nepal without informing the government.

The debate in India over Chinese intentions in Nepal sharpened, with some analysts detecting Beijing's underlying agenda to 'liberate' Nepal from the Indian 'hegemony'. Whether China might move too far and too fast and risk a backlash from India was now being debated against the willingness of New Delhi to identify with the US rebalancing in the Asia-Pacific. Nepalese officials continued to insist that Upadhyaya's recall was unrelated to the postponement of Bhandari's visit. Political events took an ominous turn.

As Oli's aides stepped up their accusations against India, Dahal declared his readiness to head a national unity government. The Maoist leader withdrew his party's support from the Oli government, but reversed course the following day. Although Dahal attributed the turnaround to the complicated political situation, some sources claimed China had been actively working to ensure Oli's continuity. A leader of a fringe party in the coalition quoted a Chinese diplomat as saying that Oli's continuation would be suitable for Nepal's stability. Chinese diplomats, according to another report, had advised top Maoist and CPN-UML leaders that Oli's departure would send the message that no Nepalese leader who sought closer relations with Beijing could expect to survive in office long. The Chinese were also said to be anxious to see Oli in office should President Xi Jinping decide to stop over in Kathmandu on his way to the BRICS Summit in Goa in October. If true, these reports underscored the extent to which Beijing had shed its traditional qualms over openly picking sides in Nepal's politics.

The political crises appeared to have eased as Oli and Dahal signed a deal that included a provision against pursuing wartime cases against the Maoists, something the former rebels had increasingly come to fear. Informally, Oli agreed to hand over power to Dahal after parliament's budget session. But the deal proved short-lived. In July, nine months after coming to power, Oli resigned just before parliament was to have voted on a no-confidence motion he was certain to lose. Indian media subsequently reported that a Dahal confidant had been in Delhi lobbying support for his premiership. It was a reflection of the changed circumstances that India, instrumental in Dahal's ouster in 2008, now greeted the prospect of his return with a sense of relief. Many Nepalese, too, saw Oli's resignation as a victory for India, but they also began weighing Beijing's possible answer to this apparent snub.

The UCPN-Maoist-led coalition took office to confront heightened public apathy. Few earthquake victims had received promised government help amid sluggish reconstruction efforts. Memories of 1990s-style unstable coalitions resting on shady compromises returned. Anxious to balance Nepal's relations with its powerful neighbours, Dahal sent his two deputies to Beijing and New Delhi. Deputy Prime Minister Krishna Bahadur Mahara sought to assure Premier Li Keqiang that Nepal accorded China priority in its foreign relations and would strengthen coordination and cooperation. Foreign Minister Wang Yi told Mahara that political changes in Nepal would not affect China's policy. In New Delhi, Deputy Prime Minister Bimalendra Nidhi met External Affairs Minister

Sushma Swaraj and Home Minister Rajnath Singh to make similar pledges.

Course Correction

New Delhi saw the beginnings of a course correction in mid-September when Dahal paid what he called a 'fully satisfied' four-day visit to India. The new premier said he held talks with Modi with 'an open heart' that allowed both countries to find fresh ways of moving forward. Critics in Nepal attacked the joint statement for its apparent pro-Indian tilt, with Oli denouncing the Dahal government's 'submission'. Dahal also faced criticism within his party, as Narayan Kaji Shrestha warned that Dahal's action in Delhi would make Nepal's other neighbour 'angry'.

Shrestha appeared to have read the Chinese mind correctly. "It looks like the bilateral relationship between China and Nepal has suddenly turned fragile and sensitive," wrote one leading Chinese expert on South Asia. "Obviously, China feels tricked. When Kathmandu needed Beijing to relieve pressure from New Delhi, it got close to China and signed a series of crucial agreements with Beijing which would help Nepal get rid of its reliance on India," he continued. "But once India's attitude towards Kathmandu relaxed a bit and the former made some promises to the latter, Nepalese politicians immediately put the nation's ties with China on the back burner." (Xu, 2016) Chinese analysts conceded that Nepal might not have taken a deliberate decision to treat Beijing as a tool to counterbalance New Delhi. Still, in their view, Nepalese politicians' short-sighted motives were influencing the course and content of Beijing-Kathmandu relations.

The mood shifted somewhat as Dahal met with President Xi on the sidelines of the BRICS-BIMSTEC outreach summit in Goa. Discussions focused on scheduling the Chinese leader's long-awaited visit to Nepal and ways of implementing the agreements the two countries had already signed. Then Dahal and Xi found themselves huddled in an unscheduled informal three-way summit after Modi happened to 'drop in'. Dahal proposed ways of enhancing trilateral strategic cooperation and partnership, reminding the Indian and Chinese leaders that he had proposed so during his first premiership in 2008. Beijing had welcomed the proposal then, while India offered no response. Dahal told reporters in Kathmandu that he found both India and China positive this time. When it saw the Goa meeting being publicised as the onset of trilateral cooperation – something New Delhi had never warmed up to – the Ministry of External Affairs stated that the Modi-Xi-Dahal encounter had not been a trilateral one in the traditional sense.

Nepal-India relations still headed in a positive direction. Pranab Mukherjee's arrival in Kathmandu in early November marked the first visit by a President of India in 18 years. He held a series of meetings with political figures both from the ruling and opposition parties as well as disgruntled Madhesi groups. Mukherjee also visited Pashupatinath Temple in Kathmandu and Ram Sita Temple in Janakpur and addressed a symposium on Nepal-India relations. Closely involved in India's Nepal policy as a minister under successive Indian prime ministers, Mukherjee had played a leading role in bringing Nepal's Maoists into the democratic process. Since he was visiting Nepal in a ceremonial capacity this time, there were few expectations of a breakthrough. Still, Mukherjee's reiteration of the Modi government's support for a new constitutional amendment to address Madhesi demands prompted criticism of unwarranted interference.

The constitution amendment bill before parliament had sharply polarised politics. The main opposition CPN-UML warned that the bill's proposal to segregate the hills and plains districts and ethnic groups from proposed provinces No. 4 and 5 – so numbered because of the parties' inability to name them – but Dahal refused to withdraw the measure. Former King Gyanendra, who had become more candid in his recent public pronouncements, called upon the people to save the country from an onslaught on its unity and integrity. As the government announced Nepal's first local elections in two decades, Madhesi groups vowed to oppose it unless the Constitution was amended first.

Demands for a reassessment of Nepalese foreign policy in terms of articulation, goal-setting and execution began to grow in academic and media circles in Kathmandu. Replacing the traditional 'balanced diplomacy' with country-specific strategies, bolstered by credible governance, was regarded as vital to reassure India and China about their genuine security concerns. Yet traditional diplomacy continued to hold sway. Prime Minister Dahal left on an official visit to China in March 2017 to take part in the Boao Asia Forum and hold discussions with President Xi Jinping. Although Nepal had prepared five agreements, Dahal did not sign any. Analysts detected deep Chinese suspicions, as President Xi urged Dahal to enhance trust and work more actively on implementing past agreements. Chinese analysts had been complaining of Kathmandu's waning interest in the deals Oli had signed, including Nepal's commitment to joining China's One Belt One Road (OBOR) project. Underscoring the depth of their displeasure, Chinese sources also let it be known that Xi had cancelled his visit to Nepal at the last hour in October and instead visited Bangladesh.

Back home, Dahal said Nepal would formally sign a memorandum of understanding with China on becoming part of the OBOR initiative at the earliest. Nepal was also keen to develop cross-border roads, railways, transmission lines and industrial parks in cooperation with China. Like India, but more indirectly, China began pressing Dahal to address Nepal's political uncertainty by taking all sides on board.

India's new ambassador, Manjeev Singh Puri, arrived in Kathmandu conveying the message that New Delhi would be more closely engaged in Nepal's development. He indicated India's interest in building a 76-km fast track that would link Kathmandu with Nijgadh in the Terai along with an international airport at Nijgadh. Ominously, a week later, the government entrusted the $900 million-plus project to the Nepal Army instead. Both neighbours seemed to have decided to tighten the screws on Nepal at the same time.

Indian Army Chief General Bipin Rawat visited Nepal to receive the title of 'Honorary General' of the Nepal Army, a reciprocal arrangement between the two countries since 1965, and assured extensive cooperation to further the traditional ties between the two armies. By this time, there seemed to be greater Indian acknowledgement that the Nepal Army's growing engagement with China was a direct outcome of New Delhi's support to the Maoists in 2005-2006. In mid-April, China and Nepal began their first-ever joint military exercises focusing on counterterrorism, a follow-up to the visit of Chinese Defence Minister Chang Wanquan the previous month. Domestically, the government underscored the importance of the exercise, while Nepalese Embassy officials in New Delhi were playing down its strategic significance.

Paying a long-delayed visit to India, President Bhandari held talks with President Mukherjee, Prime Minister Modi and leaders of various political parties. They renewed their commitment to enhancing all aspects of bilateral relations. New Delhi reiterated its position on the need for a broader-based Nepalese Constitution. Amid the ongoing tussle between the Madhesi groups and the Dahal government, New Delhi assured all assistance to Nepal for the upcoming local elections. India felt it had to tread carefully between the imperatives of advancing the democratic process and supporting the legitimate grievances of the Madhesis.

Nepal held its first local-level elections in 20 years in May and June over three phases, recording a turnout of up to 78 percent. The CPN-UML won the most seats in all four categories, with 294 of its candidates becoming mayors, 331 deputy mayors, 2,560 ward chairs, and 10,912 ward members. The Nepali Congress came in second in all four categories and the CPN-Maoist Centre third. Overall, 18 different parties captured local level seats.

Before the first legislative elections under the new Constitution, Nepal underwent an informal prime ministerial transfer from the Maoists to the Nepali Congress as part of the power-sharing deal struck after Oli's resignation. Dahal's UCPN-Maoist had merged with two other factions to become the CPN-Maoist Centre before he handed over the premiership to Sher Bahadur Deuba. Indian critics of Dahal's first term as premier appeared satisfied with his latest performance.

They saw him build bridges with the Madhesis and the janjatis by promising a consultative process and a constitutional amendment addressing their concerns and lauded Dahal's efforts in repairing relations with India that had soured under Oli.

As Deuba took office, the standoff between India and China at their tri-junction border point with Bhutan on the Doklam plateau had cast its shadow on Nepal. A CPN-UML lawmaker pressed the government to clarify its stance, citing the loss Nepal would suffer in case of a full-blown conflict. Nepal refrained from commenting on the issue, saying it was a bilateral one between India and China.

The flurry of visits from India and China continued as Indian External Affairs Minister Swaraj attended a multilateral conference in Kathmandu in early August, days before Nepal hosted Chinese Vice Premier Wang Yang. Deputy Prime Minister Krishna Bahadur Mahara affirmed that Nepal would not take sides in the Doklam standoff. During a meeting with Deuba, Swaraj sought to dispel the image of India as an external micro-manager. She advised Madhesi leaders to focus on the provincial and national polls.

During Wang's visit, Nepal and China signed three important agreements encompassing a wide range of projects, including a feasibility study on natural gas and petroleum products. The other two areas related to hydropower projects and transmission lines and economic and technological cooperation. Nepal won Chinese assurances on reopening the Araniko Highway following the earthquake-induced obstruction, with Beijing also agreeing to upgrade the vital road.

Indian media reaction to growing Chinese involvement in Nepal remained mixed. Some still saw Chinese aid as a tool of fomenting anti-Indian sentiments in Nepal, while others considered Nepal uniquely placed to mediate on Doklam (Ghosh 2017). China, too, seemed anxious to assuage Indian concerns. As Deuba left on a visit to India, one Chinese analyst urged new Delhi not to put "the wrong geopolitical interpretation" on economic cooperation between China and Nepal. "In recent years, China has stepped up investment as well as economic aid to Nepal to revive its ailing economy. But Beijing has no plan to turn Nepal into a battlefront to counter India," (Hu Weijia 2017). "Otherwise, it would have given far more economic aid to Nepal to persuade it to stand together with China." India should instead consider working with China in assisting Nepal, he added.

The search for a new regional equilibrium was becoming imperative. In New Delhi, both sides refused to admit officially that Nepal-China relations featured during Deuba's talks with Modi and National Security Adviser Doval. However, they did figure in other high-level meetings. Former prime minister Manmohan Singh asked Deuba whether all the big cities of Nepal were now connected with China, a suggestion Deuba denied, according to published reports. When one Indian minister raised the issue at a public function, Deuba emphasised that India should not worry about Nepal's relations with China. Members of the Nepalese delegation said they had found a softening in India's stance on the Nepalese Constitution following the Doklam standoff. Back home, Deuba was reprimanded for saying during a joint news conference with Modi that he would continue to push for amending the Constitution. The main opposition CPN-UML and ruling CPN-Maoist Centre said the premier should not have spoken about an inherently internal matter.

Deputy Prime Minister Mahara held talks with Premier Li Keqiang and other Chinese leaders in Beijing in mid-September. The two sides reiterated their commitment to work closely to enhance rail and road connectivity under China's Belt and Road Initiative (BRI, as OBOR had now been rechristened. Mahara assured the Chinese leadership of broad consensus among prominent Nepalese leaders to carry forward railway connectivity with China as a national priority project. They also agreed to carry out a technical study of the railway project. China pledged more significant support for highways, railways and cross-border transmission lines under the BRI.

Around the same time, in a separate development, China stepped up the ante on Doklam. New Delhi had been asserting that the road building at the China-India-Bhutan tri-junction in the strategic narrow Chicken's Neck area had changed the status quo. In response, Wang Wenli, Deputy Director-General of Boundary and Ocean Affairs of China's Ministry of Foreign Affairs, asked a group of Indian journalists visiting Beijing: "The Indian side has also many tri-junctions. What if we use the same excuse and enter the Kalapani region between China, India and Nepal or even into the Kashmir region between India and Pakistan?" (PTI, 2017)

Deuba, for his part, was mired in new controversies as the national elections approached. After setting the electoral calendar in motion, Deuba in September petitioned for a delay citing ballot irregularities. Deuba had acted only after the CPN-UML and CPN-Maoist Centre struck a surprise pre-electoral alliance. The CPN-Maoist Centre, a partner in Deuba's Nepali Congress-led ruling coalition, intended to unite with the CPN-UML after the election. Deuba stripped 17 Maoist ministers of their portfolios after they defied his instructions to resign. Accusing Deuba of conspiring to postpone provincial and federal elections scheduled in two phases on November 26 and December 7, the Maoists refused to quit. Deuba gave some Maoist portfolios to the royalist RPP members he had inducted earlier. Splinter Maoist groups accused Dahal of compromising on ideology by taking the party into the same parliamentary politics they had once taken up arms against.

In a sudden move, the Deuba government cancelled an agreement with a Chinese company to build the largest hydroelectric plant in the country. The 1,200 MW Budhi-Gandaki project, signed with the state-owned China Gezhouba Group Corporation, would have nearly doubled Nepal's current hydropower production and cost an estimated $2.5 billion. But the Finance Ministry recommended it to be scrapped, saying it had been awarded without a transparent bidding process. Nepal's contract rejection came as a surprise to the Chinese company, which had built the massive Three Gorges Dam. A Chinese Foreign Ministry spokesman in Beijing said the news had come as a surprise. CPN-UML chairman Oli criticised the act calling it a government ploy to raise money for poll expenses from rival investors. CPN-Maoist Centre chairman Dahal, under whose government the deal had been sealed, called a decision a blunder.

The move was seen as a setback to China at a time it was

already confronting project cancellations in other parts of South and Southeast Asia. Dismayed by India's perceived role in ousting the Oli government, Beijing had voiced concern over the apathy by successor governments in Kathmandu to implement past agreements. Chinese media noted that Beijing had later included the Budhi-Gandaki project as part of the BRI as per the Deuba government's request. One Chinese newspaper editorial suggested the hydropower project could have been cancelled in retaliation for it what it called false perceptions of Beijing's role in forging the Oli-Dahal alliance.

Despite some violent attacks by disgruntled groups, the elections were deemed free and fair. Of the 275 seats in the legislature, 165 were to be filled on a single member, simple-plurality basis and 110 on closed-list, proportional representation. In the first category, the CPN-UML/CPN-Maoist Centre leftist alliance secured 116 of 165 seats, with the Nepali Congress taking 23 and the remaining 26 going to smaller parties. The second category produced a wider distribution of votes among the major parties: 41 seats for CPN-UML, 17 for the Maoist Centre, and 40 for the Nepali Congress. The Rastriya Janata Party and Federal Socialist Forum equally split the 12 remaining seats.

In contrast to the 2008 and 2013 elections, issues like political stability, economic and infrastructure development, and migration dominated the 2017 electoral debate in Nepal. Voters demanded better roads, jobs, hospitals, schools, and electricity and placed development over ideology. Cadres of both alliances in constituencies, too, sought assurances of development from their candidates. Keeping this in mind, both alliances promised rapid economic growth if voted into power.

The left alliance, led by the CPN-UML, and the democratic alliance, led by the Nepali Congress pledged rapid economic growth. They promised to develop friendly relations with both China and India in order to reap economic gains. Projecting India as an interfering neighbour, the left alliance pledged to review Nepal's 'unequal' treaties with India. The political parties' open support to the BRI over India's stated reservations indicated the overall shift in the national mood. Nepalese increasingly recognised that while India still provided easier access to transit facilities and markets, China was better placed to extend technological and financial support. If harnessing those complementarities was not possible, Nepalese appeared prepared to avoid siding with one neighbour.

If China was pleased with the election outcome, India faced the prospect of one-time ally turned foe Khadga Prasad Sharma Oli's return to power. On January 21, Prime Minister Modi telephoned Oli to congratulate him in advance and invited him to India. A week later, External Affairs Minister Swaraj landed in Kathmandu with a 'special political message' from Modi to Oli. In a gesture perceived as a softening of India's stance on the Constitution, Swaraj urged Madhesi leaders to focus on forming the government in Province No. 2, the only one the CPN-UML had not won.

Losing the Plot

A YEAR AND a half after his unceremonious exit, Khadga Prasad Sharma Oli returned to power on February 15, 2018. This time he took the oath of office as Nepal's first elected prime minister under the country's federal republican Constitution. The CPN-UML and the CPN-Maoist Centre announced their first significant step towards formal unification. For the first time, Nepal's communists – a constellation of India sceptics – enjoyed a comfortable majority in parliament. The following month Bidya Bhandari was elected president for a second term, winning over two-thirds votes from the 880-member Electoral College comprising the bicameral federal parliament and seven provincial assemblies.

Although she was only midway through her five-year first term, election law had mandated new presidential elections within a month of the first meeting of the federal parliament. As Nepalese looked forward to political stability, good governance, strengthened democracy and increased prosperity, the general thrust of the polity had already made India uncomfortable. China saw the communist electoral triumph and impending party unification as conducive to the future of bilateral relations, a sentiment that could only add to New Delhi's anxieties.

Having set out on a positive note in public, Nepal and India recognised the onerousness of the task ahead. Oli felt India had engineered his ouster for the strong nationalist stand he had adopted during the Indian embargo. The glee exhibited by sections of the Indian media at his departure then – and the willingness of some commentators to grant New Delhi credit for having ensured that – had served to heightened Nepalese suspicions. So, Oli partly owed his latest triumph to public perceptions of Indian victimhood. On a visit to India in early April, Oli sought to put such bitterness behind. Focusing on the imperative of fulfilling mutual economic aspirations. Oli nevertheless sought greater respect from New Delhi for sovereign decisions Nepal took vis-à-vis the rest of the world.

Oli and Prime Minister Narendra Modi pledged to expand bilateral ties in all areas, especially in development cooperation, trade and investment, agriculture, energy, connectivity and people-to-people contacts. Remotely inaugurating the Integrated Check Post at Birgunj in Nepal, the two premiers hoped the facility would enhance cross-border trade and transit and shared growth. Oli and Modi also witnessed the ground-breaking ceremony of the Motihari-Amlekhgunj cross-border petroleum pipeline.

Officials insisted China did not figure during the talks, although regional issues such as BIMSTEC and SAARC did come up. Still, speculation centred on why the two leaders had not inaugurated the Arun-III hydroelectric power project.

At a public reception, Oli addressed the question of Nepal's growing proximity with China: "We are a country with two big neighbours…. Friendship is the starting point of our foreign policy, our neighbourhood policy."

Widening that neighbourhood became a centrepiece of Foreign Minister Pradeep Gyawali's talks in Beijing later in the month. At a joint press conference, Chinese Foreign Minister Wang said China and India should develop a consensus on supporting Nepal's development. Acknowledging India's reservations on trilateral cooperation, Wang said Nepal hoped to give play to its geographical advantages and serve as the bridge and bond between China and India so to benefit from the development of both. Beijing and New Delhi should be jointly supporting what he called Nepal's 'reasonable and justifiable' wish.

Modi visited Nepal in mid-May against the background of fresh rapprochement efforts by India and China. He described himself as having arrived on his third visit to Nepal in four years as 'Prime Pilgrim'. The two-day trip had all the trappings of traditional diplomacy. Be they at temples, felicitation ceremonies, or official talk venues, Modi used the right words and gestures to win over Nepalese still bruised by India's unofficial blockade in 2015-2016. Officially a state visit, Oli deployed the full administrative machinery to ensure Modi felt welcome. He left with generous pledges of support to Nepal in terms of specific projects and general commitments of more.

Many in both countries saw Modi's visit as part of an effort to shore up his Hindu nationalist Bharatiya Janata Party (BJP)'s prospects ahead of crucial national elections the following year. Still, the trip embodied the dynamics of politics, religion, economics and culture underpinning bilateral relations. Modi's affirmation that Nepal remained the first neighbour in India's 'neighbourhood first' policy sounded reassuring. Oli came in for much criticism for appearing with Modi in Janakpur in matching traditional Indian garb instead of Nepalese attire. Overtures to India came with risks.

Maintaining Nepal's deft balancing act, Oli visited China in June. The two countries agreed to execute several projects within China's Belt and Road Initiative (BRI) and outside. They also advanced a feasibility study for the Kerung-Kathmandu railway link, which an official joint statement described as "the most significant initiative in the history of bilateral cooperation". Nepal and China also agreed to strengthen cooperation between law enforcement agencies on information exchanges, capacity building and training. They agreed to negotiate treaties on mutual legal assistance in criminal matters and extradition and reiterated their firm commitment to respect each other's sovereignty and territorial integrity.

Chinese media commentary during Oli's visit focused on the need to establish a benign China-Nepal-India relationship. Chinese analysts urged India to be confident that Nepal would not turn its back on New Delhi howsoever well it got along with China. Recalling that during Indian Prime Minister Modi's visit to China in May 2015, President Xi had proposed a China-Nepal-India Economic Corridor (CNIEC), which New Delhi ignored. The Wuhan meeting earlier in the year had significantly improved Sino-Indian trust, which brightened the prospects of the CNIEC. The corridor, in Beijing's view, would not only facilitate Nepal's development but would also make the country a bridge between China and India to create opportunities for northern India.

Overall, New Delhi appeared satisfied. "It speaks to where bilateral relations are now that Oli's five-day official visit to Beijing last week has not set off panic in India," one newspaper editorial commented. (Indian Express, 2018). "Instead of agonising over what China is doing in Nepal, Delhi would do well to fast-track the delivery on its own commitments to its Himalayan neighbour." While the '2+1' formula did not seem to gain traction in New Delhi, hopes for Nepal relations grew later in the month. After nine rounds of meetings and more than two years of deliberations, the Eminent Persons Group finalised a joint report that would be submitted to the prime ministers of India and Nepal. Although non-binding, the recommendations were expected to contribute to updating bilateral relations comprehensively in keeping with the times.

Nepal focused on regional diplomacy in late August as the host of the fourth summit of the BIMSTEC. The meeting drew the participation of Modi and the leaders of the other five member states. Adopting an 18-point declaration, the leaders underlined the importance of multidimensional connectivity as a key enabler to economic integration for shared prosperity of the region. The declaration also highlighted the importance of trade and investment in fostering the region's economic and social development. Barely a week later, Nepal surprised fellow members by pulling out from a scheduled joint BIMSTEC military exercise in the Indian city of Pune. Prime Minister Oli's explanation to Indian ambassador Puri that he was forced to act under immense political pressure did little to assuage New Delhi, especially when Nepal had one of its strongest governments ever.

Also in September, Kathmandu and Beijing completed the text of the much-awaited protocol of the Transit and Transportation Agreement that would allow Nepal access to Chinese seaports at Tianjin, Shenzhen, Lianyungang, and Zhanjiang for third-country trade. Nepalese and Chinese teams also carried out field visits of Kurintar in Chitwan where the proposed Nepal-China rail was expected to cross as well as a new north-south corridor to be built. The agreements provided immediate political benefits to the Nepalese government and held out the promise of more massive Chinese investments.

New Delhi's bewilderment turned into displeasure when Nepal took part in Chinese-led military drills in Sichuan province. Publicly, Kathmandu insisted that it was merely exercising its sovereign choice on which military exercise to attend. Just as a cancelled Chinese project here or there could not be construed as an indictment of Beijing's massive BRI, Oli advisers appeared to suggest, the withdrawal from Indian military drills should not be automatically equated as a snub to New Delhi. The Oli government then attempted some dexterity. Days after cancelled a $1.6 billion deal with a Chinese company to build the West-Seti hydroelectric project, it reinstated the $2.5 billion Budhi Gandaki hydroelectric deal the Deuba government had scrapped before the election.

The episode underscored the threat regional rivalries posed to Nepal's development aspirations in a sector with the greatest potential. The company building the West Seti project found it financially unfeasible due to high resettlement and rehabilitation costs. However, it had wanted the Nepalese government to pull the plug. It then emerged that China had decided to pull out because of India's refusal to purchase power from the plant.

In 2016, India introduced a regulation requiring its states to purchase electricity only from companies with a 51 percent equity investment of Indian public and private companies. The Nepalese discovered that the largest potential buyer was out of the market because it did not appreciate where the investment came from (Bhattarai, 2018).

Domestically, the Oli government initially won praise for its actions against the transportation cartels, irresponsible contractors, and non-transparent and unaccountable nongovernmental organisation leaders and private-school owners. Oli also persuaded the Federal Socialist Forum, Nepal, led by Madhesi and indigenous leaders, to join the government with the promise of constitutional amendments the party demanded. The economy rested comfortably enough on work related to earthquake reconstruction and economic growth driven by remittances, tourist arrivals and an easing of power cuts. The imperative of shifting the economy from its remittance and consumption base to investment and production was becoming evident.

As the government's reforms stalled, public scepticism grew over the prosperity Oli had pledged during the election campaign. The government began coming under criticism from a variety of directions. Accusations of creeping authoritarianism rose when the government banned public protests in the Maitighar Mandala, the central venue for protests in Kathmandu. (The courts overturned the ban). Journalists protested what they saw as restrictive provisions in new media laws. Deteriorating law and order led to a plethora of media stories of rape, murder, corruption, smuggling, caste and gender discrimination, and shootings.

Disadvantaged groups accused the government of reversing the reforms begun under the 2007 interim Constitution and appointing members of the traditionally dominant ethnic groups to key posts. As the political parties led by the Madhesi formed a government in Province 2, indigenous nationalities continued expanding their social, cultural, and political movements. Oli himself was accused of using a narrow ethnonationalist outlook to bolster his politics. Many saw the government's reluctance to empower the provinces through appropriate funding and staffing as a calculated ploy to ensure the failure of federalism.

The NCP's effort to recruit, appoint, and promote party loyalists, cadres, and members from the dominant ethnic groups in the bureaucracy, police, and judiciary was seen to have enfeebled institutional autonomy. The Prime Minister's Office brought the National Investigation Department, the Department of Revenue Investigation, and the Department of Money Laundering Investigation under its purview, ostensibly to combat corruption and increase efficiency. Critics saw those agencies less likely to act against elements close to the power establishment. Factionalisation narrowed the prime minister's room for action. When Oli called on ruling party leaders and cadres to defend his government, some publicly refused to do so.

Theoretically, the Oli government enjoyed a near-two-thirds majority. However, its efforts to centralise power fanned factionalism in the NCP. In an eerie reminder of the past, the prime beneficiary appeared to be the CPN-Maoist, which pledged to complete the revolution the original Maoists had abandoned by joining democratic politics. Led by 'Biplab', the nom de guerre of one-time Dahal loyalist Netra Bahadur

Chand, the CPN-Maoist boycotted the 2017 elections to prepare for an armed rebellion. During the campaign, it had set off over a hundred improvised explosives across the country, targeting rallies of prominent politicians. The group subsequently planted a bomb at the office of Indian-built Arun III hydropower project and attacked a tower of telecommunications giant Ncell, which owed the state over half a billion dollars in unpaid taxes.

Then came a jolt from farther afield that would set off wider geostrategic shock waves. The Nepalese learned that the United States now saw them as central to a free and open Indo-Pacific. People in the landlocked nation could easily go beyond the maritime connotations of the term and comprehend its wider geographical import. But that was little solace. Viscerally sceptical of their giant southern neighbour India, the 'Indo' part of what had become the latest international relations fad carried heavy historical baggage. The 'Pacific' side was a geographical contrivance that might be partly redeemed by its connotation to Nepal's other giant neighbour. But, then, containment of China remained the clearest implication of Washington's assertive yet ambiguous formulation.

When Foreign Minister Pradeep Gyawali returned home from suddenly scheduled talks with US Secretary of State Mike Pompeo in mid-December, he was prompted to issue a clarification. Nepal's 'central role' in a free, open, and prosperous Indo-Pacific, as the State Department stressed in its official statement after their discussions, did not pertain to geostrategy. Pompeo's focus was on how the United States saw Nepal's place in a vital geographic region.

The resumption of direct high-level contact between the

United States and Nepal after a 17-year hiatus itself was bound to generate much interest. The prevailing view in Nepal was that the United States took the sudden initiative. That, in turn, brought back memories of early 2002, when then-Secretary of State Colin Powell made a hastily scheduled stopover in Kathmandu. During that visit, Powell had primarily bypassed the elected government to discuss directly with the Nepalese monarch and generals on ways of strengthening the Royal Nepal Army's capabilities in suppressing the Maoist insurgency. Washington, like Kathmandu and New Delhi, had designated the Maoists a terrorist group.

Powell's trip paved the way for an Oval Office meeting between President George W. Bush and Prime Minister Sher Bahadur Deuba later that year. Nepal's entry into the global war on terror set in motion a chain of events that ultimately led to the abolition of the monarchy and triumph for the Maoists in multiparty elections.

Welcome as renewed American interest may have been, there were also reasons for apprehension, especially since Nepal's post-2006 political evolution primarily had been driven by Sino-Indian cooperation and conflict. Renewed American engagement with Nepal could excite India in terms of the broader contours of its relationship with the United States. Locally, it was bound to raise Indian apprehensions, as New Delhi assiduously avoided being relegated to a junior partner to Washington as well as raising Beijing's suspicions.

For China, the general ambiguity of Washington's Indo-Pacific Strategy may have been a source of satisfaction. Still, Beijing recognised it could not afford uncertainty over US and Indian intentions in Nepal amid an ageing Dalai Lama and the inevitable search for the next Tibetan leader. The 14th Dalai Lama had been living in exile in India since 1959, along with thousands of followers apprehensive of the future. The Chinese were too steeped in history to forget that Nepal once served as an important base for a US-sponsored Tibetan insurgency against China.

Such external undulations were bound to play out in Nepal's cantankerous politics. The Nepali Congress, traditionally friendly to both Washington and New Delhi, would be tempted to use any perceived deviation in Nepalese foreign policy to undermine the government. The ruling NCP would relish an opportunity to extricate itself from the India-China straitjacket. Its more radical cadres, however, were not likely to appreciate their leaders hobnobbing with 'imperialists' amid the party's factionalism. The Nepalese people, eager for tangible economic and social benefits of democracy, saw in the new US Millennium Challenge Corporation assistance offer a source of some succour and sustenance, but only if history and geography could leave them enough breathing space.

Oli hoped to expand his room for manoeuvre by widening Nepal's international engagement. In January 2019, he travelled to Switzerland, where he became the first Nepalese leader to address the Davos Summit. Stating that Nepal had recently achieved political stability, he appealed to the international community to get ready for 'deeper cooperation' in trade, investment and connectivity.

Domestic issues continued to plague him abroad. International missions in Kathmandu, led by the United Nations, sought a commitment from his government to ensure that the transitional justice process, bringing the Maoists and government together under the Comprehensive Peace Accord 12 years earlier, was taken forward seriously. The Nepalese government was asked to "clarify to the public its plans to take the transitional justice process forward in the ongoing year", according to a joint statement signed by the embassies of Australia, Germany, Finland, France, Norway, Switzerland, Britain, United States, and members of the European Union and United Nations.

From Switzerland, Oli accused the United Nations, the European Union and Kathmandu-based diplomatic missions of eight western countries of holding an ideological bias against Nepal. He called the act of issuing the joint statement "a practice of factionalism". Maintaining that Nepal's peace process was moving in the right direction, he said: "We managed the conflict and the fight is now over. Some wounds have been left, but we will cure them as well."

Back home, another controversy erupted in the form of a statement by ruling NCP co-chair Dahal criticising the United States and its allies for their intervention in the internal affairs of Venezuela. The opposition Nepali Congress slammed the NCP statement as unwarranted and injurious to Nepal-US relations, as US State Department officials in Washington sought an explanation from ambassador Arjun Karki.

Disassociating itself from the ruling party's views, the Oli government issued a far milder statement insisting that a country's internal problems should be resolved within its constitutional parameters. By the time Oli assured US ambassador Randy Berry that Dahal had 'a slip of the tongue', the Venezuela issue had widened rifts in the party between rapidly evolving pro-Chinese and pro-Indian/American factions.

Nepal appointed Nilambar Acharya as ambassador to India, filling a post vacant for over a year. A former law minister and ambassador to Sri Lanka, Acharya was a nominated member of the first constituent assembly elected in 2008 and headed its constitutional committee. Acharya was expected to put relations back on track. Although an unconnected development, C.K. Raut, a long-time secessionist campaigner, announced that he had given up his 'Free Madhes' demand. Oli welcomed Raut to peaceful politics following a Supreme Court order that freed him from imprisonment.

The deal between the government and Raut came as a surprise, not just to the public but also to leaders of the ruling NCP as well as Raut's alliance. Through an 11-point deal, Raut, coordinator of the alliance, agreed to join mainstream politics and embrace the principle of sovereignty, territorial integrity and dignity of the country as per the spirit of the Constitution. Given the extremeness of his agenda – outright secession versus autonomy – Raut, a former computer engineer working in the United States, had been operating separately from other Madhesi groups campaigning for autonomy. Still, the term Madhes was enough to revive images of India in the Nepalese consciousness.

Enthused by having brought one disgruntled group into the mainstream, the government declared 'Biplab''s NCP-Maoist a criminal group and banned its activities. Government sources insisted the intention was to apply enough pressure on the hardline Maoist group to begin talks. Alarmed independent politicians, civil society activists and human rights campaigners urged the government to make other honest efforts to invite such opposition groups for talks and undertake massive reforms to address inequalities that fuelled violent discontent. Others saw in the ban another sign of the government's growing authoritarian tendencies.

The spotlight shifted abroad with President Bhandari's visit to Beijing in April, where the Chinese government included a cross-border railway line connecting to Nepal as a project under the BRI. Although China had consented in principle to Nepal's proposal for the project, it was yet to clarify how it would be carried out. The Chinese were thought to be seeking a firmer commitment from Nepal to the BRI. In Kathmandu, Chinese ambassador Hou Yanqi insisted that the BRI would not put Nepal or any country in a debt trap. Businesses, as the leading players in BRI cooperation, would act according to the law of the market to ensure they did not lose money. Most developing countries needed funds for development and China, as other international financial institutions did, offered help. It did so based on equal consultation and attaching no additional political condition. That way, Hou insisted, the BRI would help some countries come out of the trap they were already in (Huang Ge, 2019).

Two months later, Prime Minister Oli attended the swearing-in ceremony of Narendra Modi in New Delhi as he assumed a second term as premier. In their meeting, the two leaders expressed their commitment to further deepening relations, in particular between the peoples. Modi's massive re-election in May spawned concern that right-wing Indian groups could step up their campaign to restore Nepal's Hindu statehood and perhaps even the monarchy. Under Modi's first term, former King Gyanendra had made several private visits to India where he also met with leading ruling party and opposition leaders. Traditional Hindu groups continued to felicitate him the Hindu king at Indian temples and religious conclaves. The election of a leading Hindu pro-monarchist ascetic in the BJP as chief minister of the crucial Indian state of Uttar Pradesh along Nepal's border, had enthused Hindu and pro-monarchy groups on the fringes of Nepalese political life.

Suspicions of the Modi government's intentions in Nepal during its second term grew in mid-July when the new chief of India's external intelligence agency RAW arrived in Kathmandu and held extensive talks across the political establishment. Media reports detailed the specifics the RAW chief ostensibly discussed with each prominent Nepalese politician, who in turn were busy denying any such meeting. The appointment of S. Jaishankar as foreign minister, whom many Nepalese remembered as the foreign secretary Modi had sent to delay the promulgation of the Constitution in 2015, brought back memories of the unofficial blockade.

Another growing concern was the Modi government's continued 'inability' to receive the bilateral Eminent Persons Group report on ways of modernising relations. The appointment of Bhagat Singh Koshyari, the coordinator from the Indian side, as the governor of Maharashtra added to Nepalese concerns. Kathmandu had considered Koshyari, given his influence in the ruling party, the only person capable of pushing India's acceptance of the report, which suggested replacing the 1950 Treaty of Peace and Friendship and regulating the open border. While the Oli administration had prioritised execution of the report, Modi government sources cited the prime minister's busy schedule for his inability to receive the report.

Initially, the general election in India was seen as the cause of the delay. Media reports in Kathmandu now attributed New Delhi's reluctance to the report's contents. The EPG proposed a 'smart border' and suggested both sides to introduce identity card for those who cross the border. The EPG also recommended limiting cross-border movements only through designated points to check infiltration, curb criminal activities, and maintain records of people travelling on either side of the border. Sceptical Indian security and diplomatic officials saw the EPG report vague on the 'smart border'. New Delhi was also concerned that Madhesis were not taken on board while forming the group and throughout the consultation process.

China, too, was becoming a growing source of public concern with the rise in criminal activities by its nationals in Nepal. After the 1962 Sino-Indian border war, a few Chinese businesspeople in Calcutta migrated to Nepal for safety. They opened Chinese restaurants in Kathmandu and settled there permanently. In the 1960s, Chinese technicians and workers started coming to Nepal as part of China-funded projects. In the mid-1990s, private Chinese contractors started bringing Chinese technicians and workers for projects in Nepal. Since 2001, Chinese entrepreneurs had ventured into private industries, businesses and travel agencies in Nepal. The trend had been growing as Chinese nationals began operating private firms in Nepal on Nepalese business visas. To cater to the growing number of Chinese tourists, the number of Chinese restaurants in Kathmandu, Pokhara and other cities had grown.

The darker side of growing people-to-people contacts had been coming into sharper focus by increasing reports of hacking, gold smuggling and women trafficking linked to

Chinese nationals in Nepal. The Nepal Police had rounded up six Chinese for allegedly hacking the security system and withdrawing millions of rupees from various ATM booths. Days earlier, four Chinese nationals were arrested for alleged involvement in a 'bride trafficking' racket. Customs officials at Kathmandu airport reported an increase in the arrests of Chinese nationals trying to smuggle gold into the country. Chinese smugglers using the Tatopani border lost that route after the extensive damage suffered in the 2015 earthquake. Many Chinese criminals had now moved operations to the Rasuwa-Kerung border crossing.

For its part, Beijing was careful to promote a message of cooperation as Foreign Minister Wang Yi arrived in Kathmandu for talks in September. The two countries signed agreements on building a hospital in Manang, relief supplies and Chinese volunteers to teach Mandarin in Nepalese schools. The day Wang left, India and Nepal officially opened South Asia's first cross-border oil pipeline. Prime Ministers Oli and Modi joined the inauguration ceremony by video link from their respective capitals. The $45 million India-funded project, with an annual capacity of 2 million metric tonnes, would enable Nepal to import fuel from India at a lower cost. The 69-km pipeline, built by state-owned Indian Oil Corporation in cooperation with Nepal Oil Corporation, was completed 15 months early.

'Bodies and Bones'

President Xi Jinping visited Kathmandu in October, marking the first visit by a Chinese head of state in 23 years. Kathmandu was the last South Asian capital Xi visited since assuming the presidency six years ago. (Bhutan, under India's tight overlordship, did not qualify as a viable destination for a Chinese president.) Significantly, Xi landed in Kathmandu after holding an informal summit with Modi in southern India. Although Beijing and New Delhi remain tight-lipped on the place Nepal occupied in the bilateral agenda, post-visit comments in both capitals spoke of a new era of trilateral cooperation between China and India and Nepal.

Oli affirmed his government's support for the BRI more persuasively. Despite India's continued reservations on the ambitious Chinese project, New Delhi recognised the value of Beijing-built infrastructure that would bolster Sino-Indian trade and commerce through Nepal. While Kathmandu declined to accede to a formal extradition treaty with Beijing, it did sign a treaty on mutual legal assistance, a thinly veiled substitute.

Globally, the comments that got the widest play were Xi's warning that anyone who attempted to split any region from China would perish, "with their bodies smashed and bones ground to powder". Naturally, many were quick to link that warning to the protests in Hong Kong. If Xi had Tibet in mind, others wondered, why he would issue that warning in Nepal, which has consistently refused the Dalai Lama entry, and not in India which hosts the Tibetan leader as well as the Tibetan government in exile?

For the Nepalese, there was an additional mystery. That section of Xi's public pronouncements in Kathmandu was not conveyed by his official interpreter. The warning came in a Chinese Foreign Ministry statement issued in Beijing. But, then, considering that very little is unscripted in Chinese officialdom, maybe that was a message from Beijing to third countries not to use Nepal's instability and flux to foment unrest in Tibet amid the Dalai Lama's advancing age and inevitable succession. Others speculated that Xi was reacting to Nepal's last-minute refusal to sign the bilateral extradition treaty for fear of the international backlash.

Reports said the government declined Xi's request for a meeting with former King Gyanendra much in the same way it had refused Modi five years earlier. However, a leading unidentified Xi adviser held talks with the monarch as the Chinese president attended state events. Unofficial reports said senior Chinese officials were in regular consultations with the former monarch in Kathmandu and during his visits abroad.

Caught between the BRI and the US Indo-Pacific Strategy, Nepal posed a peculiar problem for both giant neighbours. While they had deep and entrenched strategic differences transcending those two issues, they had also worked to boost cooperation in areas considered mutually productive. More specifically, India and China realised that Nepal – through the auspices of third countries – had the potential to undermine the careful balance they had struck in their simultaneous quest for global leadership. Amid its praise for New Delhi's overall strategic autonomy in external affairs, Beijing had been careful not to challenge India's core interests in Nepal.

Any departure from that policy – at least from Nepal's vantage point – resulted from Beijing's discomfort with growing western state and non-state engagements in social re-engineering in Nepal in the name of enlightened and progressive transformation. India and China's respective emphasis on cultural nationalism would narrow their differences and find new ground for cooperation in Nepal, imbued as it was by an amalgam of Hindu and Buddhist traditions. If anything, such a Sino-Indian framework for stability – if there were one at all – could have only been in an embryonic state. Refining it into a mutually acceptable and workable mechanism became a growing imperative in a region that was becoming increasingly volatile.

Any hopes of that were dashed in November when India released a new political map reflecting its recent reorganisation of the state of Jammu and Kashmir and adjoining areas. Nepal claimed the map amounted to Indian encroachment on its territory, protesting the inclusion of the Kalapani area. The Foreign Ministry said the publication of the map when a joint ministerial commission had referred the matter to the foreign secretaries of the two sides for settlement was not proper and 'absolutely not acceptable'. New Delhi claimed that the map was aimed at clarifying the areas of Jammu and Kashmir that border Pakistan, not Nepal. The External Affairs Ministry said the new map had, in no manner, revised India's boundary with Nepal. The boundary delineation exercise with Nepal was going on under the existing mechanism.

Technically, India may have been correct. India had been depicting the disputed territories of Kalapani and adjoining areas on its map for decades. Still, the move revived an issue always politically explosive in Nepal. As public sentiment hardened against India, some Nepalese protesters also burned effigies of President Xi after reports emerged that Beijing had encroached on 36 hectares of Nepal's land. The Chinese Embassy in Kathmandu issued a strong statement refuting the allegations, recalling that China and Nepal delimited and demarcated their border under a formal bilateral treaty in 1961.

During President Xi's visit, the statement noted, the two sides signed an agreement on managing the boundary. Reiterating its willingness to strengthen cooperation with Nepal on boundary affairs, the embassy warned against attempts to undermine China-Nepal relations.

In early 2020, the election of a new speaker to replace Krishna Bahadur Mahara, forced to resign following rape allegations, was caught in the geostrategic whirlwind of the MCC compact. The MCC was established in 2002 by the US Congress to enable the developing countries to use its fund for infrastructure facilities and poverty alleviation. The United States and Nepal signed a $500 million compact – a five-year grant – in September 2017, with Kathmandu contributing an additional $130 million. Officially, the MCC's Nepal compact was designed to spur private investment and economic growth to reduce poverty, would also support regional energy connectivity in South Asia by strengthening Nepal's power sector and facilitating electricity trade with India.

The MCC had acquired military overtones as Washington described the initiative as part of the US Indo-Pacific Strategy, with rumours running wild of the imminent arrival of American soldiers and weaponry to contain China. The agreement held many asymmetric provisions, such as the ones specifying that the MCC "will prevail over the domestic laws of Nepal" and that funding could not be used to violate US law "or United States Government policy". While the Nepali Congress supported the compact and the NCP was deeply divided, many Nepalese saw such provisions as an infringement on Nepal's sovereignty.

While the MCC agreement clearly mentioned that the funding could not be used for the military, its provision of immunity for MCC staff in "all courts and tribunals of Nepal" drew instant parallels with similar undertakings Washington had sought in military agreements elsewhere. After the United States made an explicit statement that the MCC was part of its Indo-Pacific Strategy, a growing number of Nepalese perceived it as a counterweight to China's BRI. As such, it violated Nepal's constitutional commitment to non-alignment.

Rumours continued that Mahara may have been punished for his refusal to place the MCC ratification before the parliament. Human rights activists opposed the leading candidate Agni Sapkota – who was eventually elected unopposed – citing a murder case pending against him at the Supreme Court. That clamour came against international human rights organisations' criticism of Nepal's lack of progress on ensuring transitional justice. The Mahara story took another twist when a district court cleared him of rape charges, citing lack of evidence.

When the anti-corruption agency filed cases against three former ministers and 11 others on a land scandal, it prompted criticism of political bias, as defendants closest to Oli escaped the dragnet. A separate corruption allegation forced a leading Oli cabinet minister to resign. The prime minister came under attack from party rivals who accused him of lack of consultation and authoritarianism, raising fears of a party split.

As Oli appeared increasingly beleaguered in early March, he recalled Nepal's ambassador to China, Lila Mani Poudyal, months before his term was to have ended. The new ambassador, Mahendra Bahadur Pandey, a former foreign minister, was believed to be close to the rival faction in the NCP. Oli had just made foreign policy adjustments based on his party's internal political considerations. Or was there something else, including the performance of Poudyal – who was Nepal's consul-general in Lhasa during the crucial 2005-2007 period? Those questions receded as Oli went in for a second kidney transplant in a Kathmandu hospital. In view of his precarious health and the riskiness of the operation, the prime minister made an emotional address to the people. However, his failure to name an acting premier marred the political climate.

While Oli's hospitalisation provided an opportunity for rival factions in the ruling party to regroup, India's new ambassador Vinay Mohan Kwatra presented his credentials to President Bhandari and began marathon meeting session with half a dozen political leaders in a day. Diplomats and politicians saw the hecticness as a portent of his term in Nepal, especially when China and the United States had both increased their engagement and visibility.

Pandemic Pandemonium

As the outbreak of the coronavirus prompted the government to ban people coming from the Middle East and the Gulf States, Iran, Turkey, Malaysia, South Korea, Japan and the whole of Europe, attention focused on the government's ability to respond to the immediate health crisis and its broader economic fallout. Oli, whose remarkable recovery from surgery surprised his doctors, ordered a lockdown and sought ways of mobilising local and regional resources. He joined Modi in a SAARC virtual summit on ways to combat the pandemic regionally. But the government's procurement order for medical supplies from China spawned allegations of irregularities. Annulling the original tender, the government authorised the Nepal Army to carry out a government-to-government procurement deal. That decision instead prompted criticism of the army's capacity in procurement and raised questions whether such purchases lay within the national defence force's mandate.

With more and more Nepalese stranded in India by the Oli government's decision to seal the borders, general confusion heightened. Oli sought to reassure an anxious nation through national broadcasts but was criticised for his often-flippant comments and his government's uncoordinated response. The crisis in governance fuelled dissatisfaction in the ruling party to the point where rivals pressed Oli to relinquish leadership of either the government or the party. A defiant Oli suddenly issued two ordinances related to political parties and the Constitutional Council, adding to his rivals' suspicions. An emergency party meeting convened to discuss the matter instead received word that President Bhandari had approved the orders.

Specifically, the ordinance related to political parties raised concerns that Oli planned to lower the threshold required for a split in the ruling party. That way, Oli could form a coalition with the Nepali Congress and endorse the MCC in parliament. When the ordinance spurred the two Madhes-based parties Rastriya Janata Party and Samajwadi Party to seal their long-pending unity, Oli withdrew the ordinances, dragging President Bhandari deeper into the party's internal rivalries.

Reports in mid-May of Indian Defence Minister Rajnath Singh inaugurating a road link via Lipulekh to Kailash Mansarovar sparked a fresh round of anti-India protests in Kathmandu. The Oli government, after some hesitation, released a new political map of Nepal that incorporated not only Kalapani but also Lipulekh and Limpiyadhura into Nepalese territory. The cabinet registered a constitutional amendment bill in parliament to revise the map in the national emblem. As these developments set the stage for a conflict with India, Washington stepped up its insistence on prompt parliamentary ratification of the MCC.

Ratification – a requirement only Nepal had made – had stalled amid deepening divisions in the ruling party. Chinese ambassador Hou Yanqi stated that Nepal was free to accept aid from anywhere it believed would promote its interests (Hou, 2020). Privately, Beijing viewed the MCC as part of the broader geostrategic rivalry the COVID-19 pandemic had sharpened. Despite being a stakeholder in the power transmission network, New Delhi had maintained a low profile and preferred Nepal to sort out the political issue to avoid irritating Beijing. With border clashes erupting between Indian and China in Ladakh, Nepal felt trapped in a tightening triangular grip. Parliament had been prorogued without the MCC's endorsement within the stipulated deadline. But moves were afoot to keep the deal alive in other ways, including an extension of the ratification deadline. That exacerbated rifts in the NCP, where an official advisory panel had recommended that the MCC should not be adopted in its existing form.

With the new map now enshrined in the Constitution with unprecedented unanimity in the legislature, the NCP factions focused on their internal rivalries. As Oli insisted he would not resign from either post, a formal party split seemed inevitable. At this point, Chinese ambassador Hou held a series of individual meetings with the rival NCP leaders as Oli and Dahal held consultations with President Bhandari on the party dispute. President Xi's telephone call to Bhandari on ways of boosting cooperation in the fight against COVID-19, too, was read in the light of the NCP dispute.

While the Modi government continued to maintain a studious silence on the map and the constitutional amendment, Indian army chief Manoj Naravane said Nepal might have raised the issue at the behest of another power, i.e. China. Although Naravane gave no evidence, his comment set the narrative for many commentators on Indian television channels. The repeated suggestion that Nepal was a puppet of China not only enraged average Nepalese but also lent credence to their lingering suspicions of the ill will lying under Indian professions of friendship.

Oli ratcheted up the rhetoric while responding to questions in parliament on the state of COVID-19 in Nepal. At one point, Oli asserted that the virus strain entering Nepal from India was deadlier than the original Chinese variant. He went on to make comments on India's national emblem that were deemed offensive. The disgust expressed by Indian TV commentators at the callousness of Oli's remark and his breach of parliamentary etiquette exacerbated the rancour in Nepal. At a public function weeks later, Oli accused his rivals in the NCP of conspiring with India to topple his government, prompting a fiery reaction in the ruling party. At yet another function, Oli claimed Lord Ram was born in Nepal and accused India of cultural encroachment.

China, anxious to build a reliable partner ever since the collapse of the monarchy, was said to have actively worked behind the scenes to unify Oli's and Dahal's parties into the NCP. Those suspicions were heightened, as the party faced its most severe rift and verged on a formal split. The NCP – like the rest of the political establishment – had united behind Oli's effort to spearhead the inclusion of a new political map in the Constitution. Privately, some NCP leaders were worried by the possible fallout from Oli's stepped-up rhetoric against India.

Dahal and Madhav Nepal made another attempt to force him to relinquish one of his two posts. The prime minister dug in his heels deeper. As a party split loomed, Chinese ambassador Hou Yanqi became active once more. The Chinese, apparently having concluded that a formal party split could allow Oli to form a coalition with the Nepali Congress to secure the parliamentary endorsement of the MCC, wanted to keep the NCP intact at all costs. That, in Beijing's view, was the best way of stalling the MCC.

As virtual workshops between the Nepalese and Chinese communist parties began drawing the participation of senior NCP leaders, Chinese Foreign Minister Wang Yi organised a video conference with counterparts from Nepal, Pakistan and Afghanistan. Officially convened to discuss ways of promoting cooperation on COVID-19, some Indians saw the embryo of a more ominous subregional quadrangle. Recognising the imperative of reengaging with India, the Oli government mobilised unofficial channels such as former ambassadors and academics.

Ending a months-long rupture in dialogue, Oli placed a congratulatory call to Modi on India's Independence Day on August 15. Modi underlined the deep civilisational ties between the two countries and urged Oli to work towards strengthening them. Two days later, Indian ambassador Vinay Kwatra held talks with Nepal's Foreign Secretary Shankar Das Bairagi on speeding up discussed India-assisted development projects in Nepal.

After months of unsuccessful attempts to meet with Foreign Secretary Harsh Vardhan Shringla, Nepal's ambassador Nilambar Acharya held talks with Ajit Doval, Modi's national security adviser. Acharya requested that a meeting of the India-Nepal Joint Commission, co-chaired by the foreign ministers, be scheduled soon. But Doval reportedly responded that a foreign minister-level meeting could take place only after official-level talks sorted out the contentious issues. Moreover, Indian sources were believed to have conveyed that anymore 'adventurism' by Nepal's ruling politicians would set back relations.

Nepal's constitutional sanction for its new territorial map exemplified the bind New Delhi found itself in Nepal. No government in Kathmandu could afford to take a step back. Amid Nepal's general political turmoil, New Delhi might detect an opportunity for replacement of a Constitution it never considered broad-based enough. A frustrated Nepalese public might support the abolition of the existing system; it would expect a successor to uphold national sovereignty and territorial integrity.

All in the Mind

IN RETROSPECT, INDIA'S bet was bold but tepid in conviction. New Delhi had brought together a plethora of players that had varying levels of commitment and vastly different definitions of success. After much behind-the-scenes prodding and cajoling, Nepal's Seven Party Alliance and the Maoists eventually agreed on a sweeping text but one they still could not sign jointly. The United States, United Kingdom and its European Union partners were united in seeking peace and stability in a geo-strategically precarious part of the world. They, too, appraised the internal partners and possibilities through different lenses. The democratic world saw New Delhi as best placed to lead the agenda for change in Nepal. But India itself was divided institutionally and ideologically over Nepal and its principal players.

The Chinese, although on the defensive, had the principal advantage of being able to act alone. That freedom allowed Beijing to adjust its Nepal policy purely on its present and projected national interests. More importantly, China, as its decades-long support for the monarchy underscored, was ideologically unconstrained. Beijing could concentrate on the contradictions of its foreign rivals and calibrate its approach to the Himalayan state in conformity with each new articulation of its rising regional and global ambitions.

India's Nepal policy, in the words of its most prominent academic on the subject, "has not always been the outcome of rational choices" (Muni, 2012). While New Delhi has sought political stability and economic well-being in Nepal through the development of its hydropower potential and a smooth flow of trade, its approach has been driven primarily to preserve and consolidate India's strategic space in Nepal. The strategic presence of extra-regional powers like the United States and traditional adversaries like China and Pakistan alike is anathema to India. Yet in 2005-2006, the internal and external dimensions of India's policymaking on Nepal clashed as much as they were compatible. New Delhi was institutionally torn. The External Affairs Ministry and the Research and Analysis Wing saw the 12-point understanding as the most viable route to peace and stability in Nepal. In contrast, the Home Ministry, the Indian Army and the domestic Intelligence Bureau, while vexed by the palace implacability, still believed in the twin pillars of constitutional monarchy and parliamentary democracy.

These multiple stakeholders were diverse and carried often mutually incompatible positions. The balance eventually struck appeared to have broadly accommodated all of them. Yet ambiguity was the adhesive. What did an end to 'autocratic monarchy' mean? Had the mainstream parties agreed to the Maoists' agenda of republicanism? Or had the Maoists accepted the monarchy? Was India a mediator that actively brought together the rival Nepalese forces or merely a facilitator of initiatives primarily driven indigenously? How would the distinction play out when the time came to implement the understanding?

An Indian-mediated agreement signed on Indian soil was bound to be toxic in Nepal, where memories of the 1950-1951 Delhi Compromise still rankled. Still, the audacity of India's ambition in 2005-2006 remained its underlying strength. Nepal's three-way conflict had deepened obstinately since a bloody palace massacre five years earlier. Now it crystallised into a bipolar one and may have become more responsive to a resolution. Internally, for India, the Naxalites had become a severe national security threat. Nudging their Nepalese cousins towards electoral democracy might have a salutary internal effect. In all this, India saw a chance to checkmate China in the small but strategic Himalayan state before the modern-day mandarins contemplated a southward expansion.

The logic was irresistible also because the counterargument had lost any appeal in the embitterment of the moment. The world's only Hindu monarch and kingdom were bound to India in a special relationship that neither country needed to define or assert. Viscerally, the Nepalese king's patronage of India's vast Hindu population was also a guarantee that the palace would not stray too far from the basic tenets of the civilisational relationship. True, Indians had seen successive Nepalese monarchs playing New Delhi off against Beijing. A little more compassion for Nepal's compulsions might have put things into sharper relief.

The idea that the deep personal and political unpopularity of

King Gyanendra became the greatest catalyst for republicanism had an alluring pithiness. But tight headlines and terse nut-graphs could not tell what was, by any measure, a far more complicated story. The palace, under King Birendra, had viewed the Maoist insurgency also as an opportunity to break out of the political straitjacket of the 1990 Constitution. The mainstream parties and the Maoist rebels, too, had been manoeuvring for advantage in the three-way split. King Gyanendra was more audacious than his murdered brother in pursuing the palace's aims. It was only when he rebuffed both the parties and the Maoists and resolved to go it alone did imperatives like peace and democracy gain wider national and international appeal and allure. The same foreign powers that enabled – and perhaps instigated – the monarch to mount his first takeover in October 2002 emerged as the fiercest critics of his second – and more sweeping – intervention in February 2005. The Chinese had not changed their stance. The singular obsession with the king's 'excesses' and the monarchy's inherently 'anti-democratic' proclivities obstructed the extrapolation of valuable pointers to an increasingly uncertain future.

Contrary to conventional wisdom, the monarchy was not always the preponderant national institution during its 240-year existence. The death of Prithvi Narayan Shah, seven years after he founded the modern Nepalese state in 1768, led to a weakening of the monarchy. A succession of minor kings left rival royal factions competing for power. Losing a third of the nation's territory in a debilitating war with the British in 1814-1816 only fuelled the feuds. From the relentless bloodletting rose the Ranas three decades later, who oversaw the eclipse of the monarchy for over a century.

Nepal's foray into modernity in the 1950s revealed the new contradictions that the newly restored monarchy would reign atop. The overthrow of the Rana regime, hailed as the dawn of democracy, ended up consolidating the powers of the palace. The inauguration of Nepal's first elected government precipitated a battle of wills in which the palace prevailed over the Nepali Congress. Royal preponderance reached its zenith during the three decades following King Mahendra's dismissal of Prime Minister B.P. Koirala's government and the abolition of multiparty democracy in 1960.

The incongruity of an impoverished nation having to finance an expensive institution was ideologically anathema to the communists. Yet the communists, whom the palace considered a counterweight to the Nepali Congress, prospered the most during 30 years of palace-led non-party rule. The Nepali Congress, which mounted unsuccessful attempts on the lives of two kings, saw a constitutional monarchy as a bulwark against a preponderance of the left.

The restoration of multiparty democracy in 1990 was expected to put Nepal irrevocably on the path of democratic modernity. Barely six years later, an avowedly republican Maoist insurgency eroded the mainstream parties and helped the palace to consolidate its position. International and regional powers, mindful of such internal contradictions, considered the palace the fulcrum of stability. India and the United States – the world's two most prominent democratic republics – joined communist China to support the monarchy.

That compact was shaken – internally and internationally – by the June 2001 Narayanhity massacre. The carnage dealt a grievous blow to the monarchy from multiple directions. It ended any halo of divinity surrounding the monarchy. The notion that the king was the guardian of the nation exploded with the bursts of gunfire. The Nepalese were reminded of the history of bloodshed and machinations associated with palace politics.

The unsavoury reputations of the new monarch and the heir apparent, coupled with swirling suspicions of their role in the palace massacre, could hardly provide a promising beginning. Yet the political parties lay discredited by their own performance, and the Maoists had little to offer politically. A wary political class and public watched King Gyanendra move to strengthen the palace's role. Still, the royal interventions of October 2002 and February 2005 failed to rouse the people into vigorous opposition. Within Nepal, the two events were considered part of a continuum. Geopolitically, they were different. The contrast revealed an essential truism of Nepalese politics. International and regional powers, with their competing interests in and expectations from Nepal, have precipitated political change based on a careful calculation of circumstances.

When King Gyanendra dismissed an elected prime minister in 2002 for not holding elections on schedule, India and the United States generally seemed content. China maintained its characteristic silence. Over the preceding years, Western governments and international donors had been growing increasingly critical of the infighting, corruption and mismanagement that had gripped the polity. Their representatives in Kathmandu had become increasingly explicit in voicing those concerns, to the point of denigrating Nepal's democracy. The 2005 royal takeover, on the other hand, instantly infuriated the Indians and Americans, while the Chinese, again, professed non-interference.

Shyam Saran arrived in Kathmandu as India's new ambassador days after King Gyanendra's 2002 intervention to promote accord between the mainstream political parties and the palace. By the 2005 royal takeover, when Saran had become foreign secretary, "what began as a valiant and mostly frustrating attempt ended with us switching to a strategy of bringing the political parties together with the Maoists to neutralise an autocratic monarchy instead" (Saran, 2018). In Nepal's telling, there is more to the story. King Gyanendra had, in fact, expressed his desire to India to take temporary control from the parties to restore peace. Nepalese political sources active during the time maintain that the monarch had sent such messages at least three times but did not hear from New Delhi (Pandey, 2015).

To the average news consumer, something did seem amiss. In the months preceding the 2005 takeover, Kathmandu and New Delhi struggled to work out a mutually convenient schedule for a royal to visit India. There was, moreover, some ambiguity on whose initiative the visit was being proposed. It was rumoured that the monarch was considering asking India to send troops to fight the Maoists. This fuelled speculation that the frequent postponements might have been intended to provide both sides sufficient opportunity to work out modalities. Sections of the Nepalese media, on the other hand, quoted palace officials as voicing surprise over the conjecture of an impending royal visit. Some Indian analysts, sympathetic to the palace, accused their own government of stonewalling.

When an official announcement of the visit finally

came, King Gyanendra's itinerary included four of the five states bordering Nepal – Uttar Pradesh, Bihar, West Bengal, Sikkim and Uttarakhand. The monarch was explicit about his intentions in an interview with a leading Indian newspaper, saying he expected to "speak my mind when in India and get to know India's perspectives on [the Maoist] insurgency" (Upadhya, 2008).

The monarch called off the visit at the last minute on December 23, 2004, following the death of former Indian prime minister P.V. Narasimha Rao. With India in mourning, that could hardly have been construed as unusual. Yet the two sides still could have used the intervening month to announce new dates. There was some speculation over whether New Delhi might have acquiesced in King Gyanendra's intervention had he named an India-friendly politician as the chairman of a multiparty council of ministers instead of assuming that role himself. Frustrated, the monarch began talks with the Maoists to bring them into the government and resolve the conflict (Adhikari, 2014). One palace source said it was at New Delhi's suggestion that the monarch became his own prime minister in what turned out to be a last-minute bid to thwart a monarchy-Maoist alliance in which India would have had no role.

The widespread public jubilation over the royal takeover was a reaction of a populace weighed down by intensifying Maoist violence and memories of the political parties' general incompetence. How myopic would the monarch have to be to institute a coup enlisting leaders of his father's generation? From the palace's perspective, the terms of the debate were wrong. What else was Nepal supposed to do when it was still fighting the 1960s-era fight of securing a geo-strategic space in a global context whose essence for the country had not changed? "If the political parties and the Maoists are both opposing [the municipal elections], my government must have made the right decision" (Upadhya, 2020) That seemed to be his regime's general approach.

Meanwhile, Beijing's anxiety was apparent. A series of palace-appointed premiers had failed to quell the Maoist insurgency, prompting greater Indian and American military involvement. New Delhi's own discomfort with American activism was palpable. Allowing the Maoists to triumph over the state would have grave implications for India's Maoist insurgency. Chinese apprehensions ran deeper. The Nepalese rebels' wholesale discrediting of Mao Zedong's reputation was intolerable enough, something the normally reticent Chinese diplomats in Kathmandu expressed with great candour. It was not hard to fathom how a total Maoist triumph could energise restive populations in the Chinese hinterland deprived of the post-Mao economic miracle.

At World Bank headquarters in Washington DC, when its Nepal office sought support for its new assistance strategy, the director representing the Chinese government promised his full backing provided that all references to the insurgents as 'Maoists' were deleted (Upadhya, 2020). The prospect of Nepal's inexorable drift toward the Indian-American camp carried grave implications for China's soft underbelly, Tibet. On the eve of the 2005 royal takeover, Nepal shut down the local offices of the principal Tibet-related organisations. The chain of events was cast easily in pro-Chinese colours.

Far from extending full support to the royal regime, however, the Chinese remained cautious. Prime Minister Wen

Jiabao dropped Nepal from his South Asian itinerary, sending his foreign minister to Kathmandu instead. King Gyanendra's expected visit to China to mark the 50th anniversary of bilateral ties did not materialise. The Indians prevented the Americans from striking a separate deal with the palace. New Delhi, for its part, was negotiating with the king. It bailed out Nepal from massive censure at the UN Human Rights Conference in Geneva and dangled the promise of a resumption of military – and perhaps even political – assistance.

A section of the Indian establishment always considered the monarchy the problem and found a propitious political alignment in New Delhi. The communist parties backing the ruling Indian coalition took the lead and moved swiftly to bring the Maoists and mainstream parties in an anti-palace alliance. The Indian army and internal security apparatus, insistent on helping the king and the Royal Nepal Army, was not pleased, as a series of leaks in the Indian media showed. This conflict emboldened the royal government, which sought to internationalise its fight against the Maoists by linking it to the global war on terror. On the ground, it went after the mainstream parties without being able to dent the rebels. New Delhi checkmated the king by facilitating a ceasefire on the eve of his attempt to raise the insurgency at the United Nations General Assembly.

The prevailing narrative was that an irate monarch responded by spearheading a campaign to secure China's position as an observer in the South Asian Association for Regional Cooperation. As that move came amid China's drive to block India from regional initiatives in East Asia, it gained instant acceptance. In New Delhi, the palace's brazen flaunting of the 'China card' hardened critics and alienated the remaining supporters of the king. The Seven Party Alliance and the Maoist rebels hurriedly signed the 12-point understanding to bring down the royal regime.

Yet sources familiar with the monarch's talks with Prime Minister Manmohan Singh always rejected that notion. The two leaders had in fact made progress on building a climate of trust critical to restoring democracy in Nepal. Sections of the New Delhi establishment sympathetic to the palace regularly cautioned their Nepalese interlocutors to be mindful of the government's coalition arithmetic (i.e., Marxist support). According to the palace version, those most impatient to push the Maoist-mainstream alliance conveniently contrived the 'China card' canard (Pandey, 2015). Hindsight allows us to take the inquiry a step further.

Could it be mere coincidence that the Indian diplomat most credited with the Indo-US civil nuclear deal was the same person who pulled New Delhi back from its traditional twin-pillar policy of supporting constitutional monarchy and parliamentary democracy? Was that what the pro-palace section in New Delhi had pointed to while cautioning Kathmandu to be sensitive to India's 'coalition arithmetic'. The Singh government won parliamentary support for the nuclear deal. The left front got to say it opposed it in keeping with India's traditional non-alignment. All it took was a legislative sleight of hand: a no-trust vote that gave both sides enough cover. Singh and the Congress party strengthened their position in elections and the left began its descent to marginalisation. If the abolition of the Nepalese monarchy was indeed the price that had to be paid, it is not even a footnote in that larger story.

It might explain Nepal's turbulent politics since.

Regardless, the peculiar collaboration between Nepal's Maoists and mainstream parties energised the Nepalese masses. The opportunity for peace and stability after years of bloodletting was too enticing to squander. As anti-palace demonstrations picked up speed, India sent a royal relative, Karan Singh, as an emissary. The king's invitation to the SPA to form the next government won instant praise from New Delhi, Washington and London. It failed to quell the protests. For the republican camp within Nepal and outside, the public defiance exposed the depth of anti-monarchism.

The collapse of the royal regime led to a swift and systematic clipping of the palace's powers. Still, a republican Nepal was not a done deal. The next phase – the suspension of the monarchy after the enactment of the interim Constitution – morphed in line with a careful power play. A precipitous de-monarchisation of the nation was precluded by the imponderables involved. The true extent of Nepalese public opinion vis-à-vis the monarchy, the loyalty of the army and the genuine extent of the Maoists' commitment to the democratic process remained unknown. What was obvious was not inspiring: the mainstream parties' poor record of governance during the last spell of democracy.

For influential international quarters, King Gyanendra became too much of a liability. He continued to insist that he had seized power in good faith, adding that the effort failed because of 'several factors'. The caveat could not have been lost on India. For the democratic West, the monarch's overt tilt toward China was inexcusable enough. His espousal of the Hinduism mantle, with a fervour surpassing that of his predecessors, was tantamount to insolence.

Had Crown Prince Paras enjoyed a better public image, forcing King Gyanendra to abdicate in favour of his son might have been an option. Passing the crown to Paras's son, Hridayendra, might have mollified royalists. For the country, it would have meant a return of the regency system. King Gyanendra, having already been crowned for a few months as a toddler in 1950-1951, understood what this implied for the monarchy as an institution. He rebuffed calls for an abdication by Prime Minister Girija Prasad Koirala and others.

Publicly, the international community shunned the monarch. Privately, they were anxious to maintain channels. One reason was China's swift move to build ties with the Maoists. The arrival of a modern high-speed train to the Tibetan capital Lhasa had greatly improved China's access to Nepal. Nepal's open border to the south exposed the Indian heartland to what many analysts there considered an enhanced military threat from China. The Terai erupted in violence against centuries of injustices inflicted by the hillspeople.

Clearly, the second amendment to the interim Constitution, which declared Nepal a republic subject to an elected assembly's ratification, was intended as a carrot and a stick for the palace. It was enough to expose the fiction that republicanism was a done deal. The king found more time to reconsider his options, as the others sought ways of remaking the monarchy in their respective images. To pre-empt any royal assertiveness, the statute also provided for the removal of the monarchy by a two-thirds majority of the interim parliament. This ultimatum failed to influence the king but vitiated the political climate. Opinion polls up to the run-up to the elections showed that half the country wanted to retain some form of monarchy. A referendum would have put the issue to rest. Perched atop that institution, King Gyanendra knew something else: elections were for presidents, not kings.

The monarchy had been central to the policies of the three major international stakeholders in Nepal. The Maoists took in royalists reportedly on the advice of the Chinese to bolster a nationalist front. A Maoist-UML alliance could go a far way toward mollifying Beijing. For New Delhi, the Nepali Congress and the three Madhesi parties could provide succour. Washington, which began its own rapprochement with the Maoists after their electoral success, saw the military as the backbone of a non-communist front. The presence of the ex-monarch within the country probably helped stabilise politics in the same way the return of Zahir Shah, Afghanistan's former king, helped the Hamid Karzai government find its footing. With the formal end of the monarchy, a new quest for internal and regional equilibrium had begun. Oddly enough, the ex-monarch was going to be a part.

Communists First

The second element of India's bet – the mainstreaming of the Maoists – represented a monumental leap of faith. On the surface, Nepalese communists were just like Indian communists – they ate, dressed, thought and sung the same way. Yet they were communists first. While appraising Marx and Engels and eulogising Lenin, Stalin and Mao, Nepalese communists were trained to denounce Indian 'expansionism' before American 'imperialism'. Age and experience might have impelled the senior leadership to make practical compromises. Still, it was imprudent for New Delhi to trust the leaders to correct the radicalism of their cadres when anti-Indianism fired up the base.

The Nepali Congress, too, drew its significance and support from within the context of a constitutional monarchy. Shorn of the crown, the party's democratic socialism would be left competing with an assortment of communists. Encouraging the Nepali Congress to break with the monarchy already meant weakening the party. Now that party was forced to confront the combined might of the Maoists and Marxist-Leninists. More broadly, in terms of China, New Delhi's new Nepal policy was based on the amity that opened up the Nathu-la Pass; it was not built for the era of Doklam and Galwan.

What India saw then was the international power balance and its regional manifestations conducive to its bet. Democracy would continue to drive the future everywhere. China, too, saw something: the imperative of calibrating its Nepal policy. While Nathu-la was good enough for the moment, the Chinese had centuries of tradition to draw upon. Mustering the flexibility for shifting circumstances was not that hard.

Breaking with tradition to welcome Koirala at the airport in New Delhi, Prime Minister Manmohan Singh called the visitor South Asia's senior statesman. Koirala, in turn, went beyond that irksome ex-monarch and called for full membership for China in the South Asian Association for Regional Cooperation. A year after the uprising, in April 2007, when it became clear the monarchy was on its way out China's new ambassador Zheng Xianglin became the first foreign envoy to present credentials to Prime Minister Koirala.

Beijing used Nepal's democratic government to mount a massive crackdown on Tibetan exiles to help turn the Beijing

Olympics into the success it became. Publicly urging Nepal to develop strong ties with India, China sought newer ways of breaking the Himalayan barrier, integrating Nepal economically and deploying it as a land bridge to the South Asian heartland well in time for the next global geostrategic realignment.

India and China were capable of joint action, though. Overcoming their sensitivities on Kashmir and Tibet, both governments supported a limited United Nations political mission (UNMIN) to assist Nepal's peace process. Once they discovered the UN was going beyond its narrow mandate, they jointly secured its removal. Neither neighbour liked the way Nepal was debating federalism. China's objections stemmed from the threats it perceived to its interests in Tibet. India felt the Nepalese models did not go far enough in extending its interests. Each competed for Nepalese hearts and minds acting on its understanding of how history and geography bound Nepal to its neighbourhood. Big brother was chastised for its embrace of estrangement. The bigger brother exuded an image of sweet reasonableness.

China promptly sent relief assistance following Nepal's 2015 earthquake. India was no less quick or generous. At the United Nations General Assembly hall in New York, Nepal's earthquake became the first test case of the Sendai Framework for Disaster Reduction adopted earlier in the year. The Chinese permanent representative matched his Indian counterpart's zeal in rhetoric and remonstrance in focusing discussions on relief every time a Western representative stood up to demand Nepal do this or that on the peace process. Relief efforts in Nepal provided China with an opportunity to train its People Armed Police for broader overseas operations. India faced a backlash for its media's often cantankerous and condescending coverage.

In Nepal, UNMIN was criticised for relying too heavily on the analysis and advice of young journalists, columnists, academics and activists with a progressive agenda. Nepalese with experience and expertise inside the UN system or in peacekeeping operations were often politely dismissed. As Kul Chandra Gautam, a former Assistant Secretary-General of the UN noted, it was only after the departure of UNMIN that the long-pending peace process, particularly the integration and rehabilitation of ex-Maoist combatants, was completed. And that, too, under a former Nepal Army general with extensive experience of commanding UN peacekeeping operations. If they wanted to, India and China could produce positive results in Nepal trilaterally.

Burdened with micromanaging Nepalese affairs while studiously denying doing so, India had the additional responsibility of looking after American interests. When the United States veered too close to the interests of its European partners on social issues, India understandably felt uncomfortable. China had the freedom to act alone. Perhaps India considered the erosion of its influence temporary and reversible over the long run. But the run kept getting longer. With new grievances joining ancient ones in the competition for global attention, an entire industry had developed in Nepal. International non-government organisations were ready to fund causes and conduct experiments that bore little relation to peace and stability. As terms like 'marginalisation' acquired broader connotations, the imperative of inclusion, too, began encompassing ever more space. Non-state political patronage in the name of freedom and democracy easily bested traditional state sources.

TRADITION WAS HARD to break in other crucial areas. Having inherited the mantle of the British Raj, independent India considered itself the protector of the weaker states in the region. The aspirations and efforts of the smaller states to develop stronger national identities were bound to clash with India's presumed political primacy.

Weak though China might have been, this contradiction opened up ever more strategic possibilities for Beijing in South Asia (Jaiswal, 2020). By the time South Asia overcame its socialist straitjacket and sought to promote economic links, China's emergence as an economic powerhouse became an attraction for the politically sensitive smaller states. Nepal found itself doubly disadvantaged. It was linked to China only through Tibet, a region Beijing has traditionally been sensitive about. China's natural expectations of Nepalese cooperation had the equally natural corollary of raising Indian suspicions. Here, too, Nepal was extremely vulnerable to punitive political, economic and other pressures India could mount at will.

From Kathmandu, sometimes the boundaries between New Delhi's domestic and foreign policies became invisible. From New Delhi's vantage point, any assertion of the Nepalese aspiration was automatically seen as anti-Indianism. As a democracy, India, like the British, enjoyed an automatic defence. Any interference in Nepal was, therefore, a contribution towards emancipating its people. During the decades of direct palace rule, nationalism compensated for the absence of popular consent. India dismissed this sentiment – and actions flowing from it – as part of an archaic and authoritarian institution's eagerness to consolidate power. To this day, some quarters in India hold the monarchy responsible for today's sour relations.

Yet New Delhi has not hesitated to coddle the palace when things have gone its way. In the early 1950s, Prime Minister Jawaharlal Nehru's faith in King Tribhuvan could last because of the monarch's personality and outlook, and the fact that he was in poor health. In King Mahendra, Nehru's foreign policy encountered a new variable in the 1960s. The palace was a source of stability, no doubt, but also an institution more willing and – given the changing regional political and security equations – better able to claim its sovereign space. As an elected prime minister in 1959, B.P. Koirala no longer resembled the young socialist revolutionary or the charming home minister Nehru once knew.

The Sino-Indian war may have compelled Nehru to engage with King Mahendra and his partyless polity. The tepidity of India's commitment to reversing that 'setback to democracy' hurt the Nepali Congress more than it helped the palace. By the time Indira Gandhi consolidated her position, she could hail King Mahendra as a poet statesman. B.P. Koirala, in exile, found it difficult even to schedule a meeting with the amiable daughter of Nehru he once knew. Even with the Zone of Peace rancour, Indira Gandhi seemed more comfortable working with King Birendra. Her son, Rajiv, saw the palace as the epitome of 'anti-Indianism'. The thaw in relations with China in the late 1980s emboldened Rajiv to reverse decades of Congress policy and avenge Mahendra's snubs to his grandfather and mother. The newly empowered democratic leadership in Nepal had good reason to be sceptical of New Delhi, despite the open Indian support they had received in overthrowing the partyless regime.

Under P.V. Narasimha Rao's Congress, the monarchy underwent another transformation. By 1993, President Shankar

Dayal Sharma could hail Birendra's sagacious stewardship, recall meeting with Mahendra but conspicuously leave out references to Nepal's three-year-old democratic triumph. In the intervening years, New Delhi witnessed difficulties in its relations with the palace. The eagerness with which some Indians still counselled their government to distinguish between the monarch and the monarchy showed the institution's broader relevance to the stability school of thought.

New Delhi was certainly entitled to espousing correlations of convenience it expected to establish and demolish at will. Whether it could manage all the variables well enough amid the region's volatility was a different matter. The temptation to hold Nepal responsible for the failure of its formulations became more untenable. If authoritarianism in Nepal has thrived on anti-Indianism, democracy has done more to fan the flames, as the 1951-1960 and 1990-2002 periods show. The swiftness with which some signatories questioned India's motives in forging the 12-point understanding between the SPA and Maoists encapsulated the crisis of confidence. This variable, it was safe to state, bore no relation to whether Nepal remained a monarchy or became a republic. What the Nepalese expected in 2006 – and still do – is the transformation of the Indian mind. If the Raj was an anachronism to Indians long before its demise in 1947, it was bound to be intolerable to the Nepalese of today.

It is not hard for Nepalese to empathise with Indians. India has remained at the forefront of Nepal's development efforts, having provided generous economic assistance in an assortment of priority areas despite its own pressing needs as a developing nation. Indian-built highways, communication systems, airports, institutions of higher learning, power stations and industries, among many other installations and facilities, have contributed significantly to Nepal's emergence as a modern state. With its vast expertise inherited from the Raj, India has trained the Nepali bureaucracy and military in modern operational procedures.

During Nepal's early years of development, the kingdom relied almost exclusively on experts and specialists trained in India. Tens of thousands of migrant workers, Gurkha soldiers and Indian Army pensioners underpinned the nascent Nepalese economy. Yet a sustained pattern of Indian policies and pronouncements has prompted many Nepalese to question the motives of Indian generosity. One analyst claims that for every rupee India has given Nepal, it has taken back Rs.771 in unfair advantage in trade and water resources (Upadhya, 2008).

Such peculiar precision might sound polemical, but it feeds Nepalese perceptions well. Indians, for their part, have been struck by the ease with which they can befriend Nepalese anywhere else in the world. They are genuinely astonished by new revelations of commonness each conversation seems to bring in third countries. Yet ordinary Indians are exasperated by the alacrity with which the Nepalese rush to blame their southern neighbour for all their problems. Long before the Gujral Doctrine of non-reciprocity in regional relations had been enunciated, many Indians considered Nepal's case a compelling antithesis.

The fallout from this perception crisis has been magnified several folds by preconceived notions and outright prejudices. As a result, such vital issues as border management, trade and transit facilities and cooperation in the crucial water sector have sunk deeper in the mire of distrust and confusion. The merits of bilateral projects hardly gain the prominence they deserve in the relevant debates. The rancour surrounding border disputes obscures the urgency of adopting modern scientific mapping to end the ambiguities. Electricity and irrigation projects become ensnared in politically charged recriminations even before their economic, environmental and engineering viability are properly gauged. Trade and transit problems acquire a sinister political complexion that clouds both the sanctity of international law as well as the benevolence of true bilateralism.

The creation of a vibrant relationship would require Nepal and India to shun this traditional mindset. That, of course, is easier said than done. Crafting a coherent alternative paradigm would require a sustained commitment to a positive relationship firmly rooted in bilateral realities and expectations. A citizenry in each country aware of the promises and perils inherent in a painstaking process could emerge as the strongest advocates of constructive cooperation.

Fanning fears of the giant southern neighbour has always been a proven political tool in Nepal. By tagging its opponents as pro-British, the Nepalese palace, as well as exiles, found it easier to make their overtures to the East India Company and, later, viceroys. After the 1951 democratic change, critics built BP Koirala into the living embodiment of pro-Indianism, and he did not seem to mind. Yet B.P. struggled to don the opposite mantle when it came time to oppose the Kosi Treaty his brother and party rival Matrika Koirala signed as premier. India's stifling embrace created the background for King Mahendra's takeover. Under him, Nepal did make significant gains in asserting its independent international identity. The Kalapani controversy and the 1965 arms agreement live on to tarnish that sound legacy.

When New Delhi imposed the trade and transit embargo in 1989, it was careful to leave open two points instead of one required under international law. Both governments knew the root of the crisis was security. If strict adherence to the 1950 Treaty was the issue, Nepal might have questioned whether India had consulted the kingdom during the 1962 war with China and the 1965 and 1971 wars with Pakistan.

After the restoration of multiparty democracy in 1990, India became a friend or adversary depending on the power equations of the day. Sometimes, the silence of the principal players vexed the Nepalese. During the height of the Tanakpur-Mahakali imbroglio in 1991-1997, the Nepali Congress chose not to discuss the issues candidly enough. Among the people, this deepened suspicions of the party's complicity with India, an accusation it has confronted from inception.

The robustness of anti-Indianism, too, has often come to haunt parties. The CPN-UML, while in opposition, promised to abrogate the 1950 Treaty and impose work permits for Indians if it ever formed a government. Once in power, it chose pragmatism. Yet its opponents portrayed the shift as a capitulation to an overbearing southern neighbour. The Maoists, who began their 'people's war' with a litany of anti-Indian grievances, fell silent during many of the anti-India efforts in the mainstream. To this day, Nepalese complaining the loudest against the iniquity of the 1950 Treaty have done little by way of explaining how they intended to dilute the political-security dimensions of a comprehensive relationship while expecting to retain benefits in other areas.

It would be unfair, however, to single out Nepal for such pandering. Convenience has encouraged India to manipulate aspects of the bilateral relationship in ways Nepal views malicious. When Prime Minister B.P. Koirala disputed Nehru's interpretation of Nepal's geostrategic position in the wake of the Chinese invasion of Tibet in 1959, he released the secret letters that had been exchanged with the 1950 Treaty. On questions relating to Nepal's freedom of import from third countries, India in 1969 leaked details of a secret arms assistance understanding New Delhi had signed with the palace four years earlier. Nepal instantly repudiated the text amid its effort to secure the withdrawal of Indian military checkposts from its border with Tibet. New Delhi, biding its time, released the full text of the understanding two decades later at the height of the dispute surrounding Nepal's arms imports from China.

During the 1979 election campaign, Indira Gandhi regularly complained of how small neighbours like Nepal had challenged India under the two successive non-Congress governments. Regardless of whether this claim helped to ensure Gandhi's post-Emergency comeback, the rest of her premiership seemed premised on an expectation of Nepalese submissiveness.

At the height of the pro-democracy protests in 1990, India had sent the draft of a comprehensive treaty on bilateral relations to the palace with the obvious quid pro quo. Sensing such a treaty would reduce Nepal's status to that of Bhutan, King Birendra rejected the draft. Palace officials suggested New Delhi had dusted off and sent to Kathmandu the same draft at the peak of the anti-palace protests in 2006.

At one point, during the height of the Tanakpur accord

controversy in the early 1990s, Indians saw Prime Minister Girija Prasad Koirala's proximity to New Delhi as a distinct liability despite the political capital he had invested in defence of the accord. After pulling out of the Dhaka summit in 2005, New Delhi publicly attributed the decision to its resolve to avoid legitimising the royal takeover. Yet privately it was assuring the United States that the pull-out was intended to convey India's displeasure with Bangladesh. (Subramanian, 2011; Panday, 2015.)

Former external affairs minister Natwar Singh, bruised by allegations of involvement in the Iraq oil-for-food scandal, used the crisis in Nepal to hit out against Prime Minister Manmohan Singh's government. Kathmandu's decision to invite the United Nations to manage arms as part of the peace process, in Natwar Singh's view, symbolised the failure of Congress diplomacy. The tendency on both sides to exploit sovereignty for domestic electoral advantage has battered the bilateral partnership.

When Sushma Swaraj, during the Ministry of External Affairs' annual press conference, said that Modi had addressed 'Indians' during his visit to Janakpur in May 2018, many Nepalese viewed her remark as another instance of India's big brother attitude. Expecting a backlash from Nepal, she quickly apologised for the mistake. During his re-election campaign in 2019, when Prime Minister Modi sought to project himself as India's chowkidar, some of his disparate critics were united in their mockery. Chowkidars, in their view, always came from Nepal.

A regurgitation of such grievances is germane to the current territorial quarrel. The Kalapani dispute's origins have been debated for decades. The Nepalese were told that King Mahendra had given away the territory for New Delhi's support. Alternatively, it was believed that India had requested and received permission from the palace for temporary defensive use of the territory around the 1962 war with China. New Delhi never responded to either suggestion, although it continues to play up unsubstantiated reports that the Nepal's monarchy had offered to merge Nepal with India after 1947. In that ambiguity, some kind of mutual arrangement might have been worked out on Kalapani. Many Nepalese were unaware of their claim all the way to Limpiyadhura until it was asserted. Given the escalation in Sino-India tensions and the region's strategic location for Indian security, India's sensitivities now must contend with hardening Nepalese sentiments.

Northern Discomfort

Sustained disregard for Nepalese grievances fuelled perceptions over time that India was attempting to delegitimise them. As a result, the territory in dispute not only ballooned in size but became so etched in Nepal's Constitution. The continued temptation to see the dispute as a Chinese-inspired ploy to weaken India on another key front is not only misguided. It is a misreading of reality, given that Nepal's own relationship with China is not free from suspicion. The Nepalese still recall Beijing's eagerness to sign the Lipulekh agreement without consulting Nepal when things were going its way (Bhattarai, 2020).

Exasperating as it is, the frequency with which Nepal feels it must reaffirm its traditional commitment on Tibet is understandable, given the context of Sino-Indian tensions. There is a growing acceptance in India that difficulties in its modern relationship with China emanate from Beijing's handling of Tibet as well as its reading of New Delhi's reaction

(Jaishankar, 2020). Yet as leading Indian analysts set out to predict dates when war with China might break out, top Indian military leaders speak of their country's readiness for simultaneous conflicts with Pakistan and China. There is a less conspicuous but certainly definite perception among some Chinese experts and analysts of an ascendance of the so-called 'confrontationist' lobby in India that sees an advantage in raising the stakes for China in Tibet. The Maoists have raised the stakes for Nepal. Regardless of whether convenience, compulsion or opportunism – or what precise mix of the three – impelled them to make a public demonstration of a drift northward, India has made no secret of its disaffection.

Such possessiveness has long irked the Chinese. Beijing believes Nepal, like every sovereign and independent country, has the right to devise its own relationship with China. As part of that effort, China regularly pledges to bolster aid and trade to lift ties with Nepal to 'a new high'. There are Nepalese who maintain China is asking too much from Nepal – i.e., subjecting itself to the full force of India's political and economic wrath – for few tangible gains. Non-conditionality in Chinese assistance loses its meaning when Beijing eternally poses the Tibet litmus test on Kathmandu.

Then there is the history of China's inability and/or unwillingness to come out in support of Nepal, especially during the 1814-16 war with British India, the 1989-90 Indian trade and transit embargo, and the April 2006 protests against King Gyanendra. In the first case, Nepal felt China was obligated to offer military support under the 1792 Treaty of Betrawati that ended the Sino-Nepalese war. In the latter two cases, the predominant dynamic was the Nepalese people's desire for democracy. However, that could not obscure the fact that Nepal's China relations were at the core of the dispute with India – Kathmandu's arms purchases from Beijing and Nepal's role in inducting China as an observer in SAARC, respectively. Even today, Maoist leader Dahal's fiery words against India have not entirely drowned out the frustration within the party over what some see as China's lukewarm support to his beleaguered government before it fell in 2008. Like grass in a field with elephants, the Nepalese need to prepare for both when they mate and fight. Nepal has been forced into its own delicate balancing. The Chinese may not sound so vociferous about it, but Beijing, too, accuses Kathmandu of flaunting the 'India card.'

If India has persisted in dismissing Nepal's concerns as a manifestation of a persecution syndrome, then perhaps the Nepalese have exhibited too many symptoms. But symptoms alone cannot promise a proper diagnosis, much less a prescription. At what point does being pro-Nepal start becoming anti-Indian? That determination becomes important since Nepalese assertiveness is here to stay as a potent political force. The temptation among some Indian analysts to conclude that, with the monarchy out of the way, this strain would disappear was as ignorant as it was inimical. In a republican Nepal, political parties, jockeying for the posts of head of government and head of state, would find it difficult to discard this established vote-getter. Nepalese parties in power may be willing conspirators in perpetuating the Raj. Unlike the Ranas, they will be free to articulate their opposition during elections.

In some subliminal way, the Nepalese find India's unwillingness to listen doubly grievous. Some British historians – certainly a minuscule portion of the community – still believe the Raj was a model of paternalistic benevolence that created the democratic and development infrastructure India thrives on today. In their collective national pride before a world paying greater attention, Indians implicitly acknowledge the integral entity the Raj created from hundreds of princely states. Deprived of the railways, education system, bureaucracy and hill stations, Nepal was left with the worst of both worlds. At a time when perceptions tend to overpower reality, dismissing Nepalese grievances as the outcome of one collective national flaw or the other would prove counterproductive. The fact that Nepalese soldiers helped the British Raj suppress the first war of independence (Sepoy Mutiny) is a fact of history. But far more Nepalese civilians shed far more blood in the movement that actually freed India.

INDIA'S AREA, POPULATION and vast accessible geographical contiguity will always make it the significant factor in Nepal. Given the preponderance of security as a core tenet of India's domestic and foreign policies, some assertiveness is perhaps built into New Delhi's outlook on Nepal. Since 'anti-Indianism' has struck deep roots in Nepal because of the way relations have been mismanaged, there is hope for a correction. Beneath the deep fog of distrust, the preconditions for a vibrant partnership do exist.

A new generation has emerged in both countries willing to acknowledge their differences and accentuate their compatibilities. For three decades after independence, the political leadership in India comprised people associated with the Indian National Congress or those espousing similar socialist beliefs. Many came from Uttar Pradesh and Bihar, carrying preconceived notions of the hillspeople from up north. Many Nepalese leaders, on the other hand, studied in such north Indian cities as Benares, Allahabad and Calcutta; some were even born in India. Their natural identification with Indian political ethos and attitudes became doubly disadvantageous. It constricted their ability to act as leaders of an independent and sovereign nation. Furthermore, these leaders were perceived as being easily susceptible to Indian pressures.

India's inconsistent policies and conflicting priorities today have coincided with the emergence of a new generation of Nepalese politicians, bureaucrats and opinion makers who are exposed to the West or have little emotional connections with India. Although it may look like India's leverage in Nepal's internal politics has eroded to its most insignificant level, it need not be an exclusive cause for handwringing. This attitudinal transformation becomes more relevant amid the economic and cultural potential inherent in the bilateral partnership. The tremendous progress India has made in information technology, developing itself as an outsourcing market for the United States and Western Europe, has inspired younger Nepalese.

Indian experts have acknowledged how Nepal's strengths – low-cost locations, cheap labour cost, and easily trainable workforce – have created room for greater cooperation. Nepal is an attractive destination for Indian pilgrims to Pashupati and sightseers. An increasing number of young Indians arrive for honeymoons and adventures. Nepal could attract more Indians seeking solace from the summer heat. With Nepalese making slow but steady inroads in Bollywood, literature and sports, Indians are acknowledging the broader potential of their northern neighbours.

Constituencies inimical to peaceful ties will persist; some as instigators, many others susceptible to manipulation. A future-looking partnership cannot proceed outside – for lack of a better term – the 'anti-Indianism' in Nepal. The phenomenon is for real, not one organisation's or individual's passport to power. No amount of Indian aid or concessions is likely to be accepted as a gesture of good faith if this perceptual dissonance dominates. Complementarities cannot amount to much if the basic nature of the relationship still is ambiguous. Even the most hawkish Indians probably recognise that their ability to 'Sikkimise' or 'Bhutanise' Nepal in the traditional sense has vastly diminished. Intellectually, their commitment to a final solution may have not. Intervention by invoking the right to self-defence is still a growing possibility should Nepal plunge deeper into crisis. Yet the costs of such a venture are mounting by the minute.

Deliberate or otherwise, Kathmandu may have widened its options through this accumulation of external interests, but it has not overcome its basic geographical constraint which leaves it susceptible to overwhelming Indian punitive pressure. Nepal's prevailing political culture has not helped fortify itself. As political forces take turns courting and castigating India, it has become far easier for New Delhi to undermine Nepal's real grievances.

Two generations of Nepalese have seen China as a benign influence. What pressures Beijing may have exerted in private in the past is best known to the palace. Privately, Nepalese leaders often voice exasperation with the conduct of their Chinese counterparts, but none match the public candour reserved for Indian politicians and bureaucrats. Should China's public affirmations to uphold Nepalese sovereignty and independence become monotonous to the point of triteness, Nepalese scepticism could lead in the opposite direction. Admittedly, this will not be enough to counteract the far deeper distrust of India. Growing acknowledgement of Nepal's strategic vulnerability, however, might make the Nepalese more understanding of their own interests. In this hazy zone, a new regional shadow play began. That may be why barely a year after his ouster, India seemed to have recognised the salutary effect of the ex-monarch's continued presence in his former kingdom.

Strategic Dissonance

The US-Indian 'strategic partnership' has been 'emerging' for so long now that its influence on Nepal has ceased to be predictable. In the palace massacre's aftermath, Washington and New Delhi showed a broad convergence of views in seeking to prevent a Maoist takeover. As King Gyanendra's takeover deepened the crisis, India and the United States calibrated their approach to prevent China from gaining a strategic initiative in the kingdom. To that extent, Washington virtually gave New Delhi a free hand in devising a political settlement. Still, New Delhi had to drag Washington away from its traditional support to the palace towards blindly accepting the Maoists' sincerity as a peace partner.

From the early 1950s, concerns about growing Chinese influence in Nepal have affected US-India relations. When, a month after the Chinese moved into Tibet in October 1950, King Tribhuvan and almost the entire royal family sought asylum in the Indian Embassy and were flown into New Delhi,

Nepal's Rana rulers deposed Tribhuvan and enthroned his toddler grandson, Gyanendra. Kathmandu immediately urged India, Britain and the United States – the three countries with which it had diplomatic relations – to recognise the new king, the only male successor left behind.

Nehru accorded Tribhuvan honours due the head of a sovereign state and continued to recognise him as king. London seemed prepared to recognise Gyanendra because the Rana regime was firmly established and in effective control of the country. However, the cabinet was split between those unwilling to go against the Indians, who were better positioned to recognise the realities on the ground, and those who were against India treating Nepal as a satellite state. London sought to mobilise the Americans to put pressure on Nehru. London and Washington eventually followed New Delhi. The result was the so-called 'Delhi Compromise' of February 7, 1951, under which King Tribhuvan, the Ranas and the Nepali Congress agreed to form a coalition cabinet that would operate under the general supervision of the monarch (Upadhya, 2012).

Still, India continued to oppose US involvement in Nepal, partly because Delhi believed that would increase Chinese interest in the country. Nehru had even suggested to the Nepalese king that he should restrict American activities. This attitude, however, changed once it had become clear in mid-1955 that China and Nepal were going to set up relations. In any case, it was becoming harder for India to aid Nepal because of its deteriorating fiscal situation. Despite opposition from its ambassador in Nepal, India had later accepted and even welcomed US involvement in certain crucial projects in Nepal. Nehru agreed to coordination between Nepal, India and the

United States, but with care so that China would not become suspicious of India's motives (Madan, 2020). As New Delhi and Washington entered a phase of mutual distrust owing to such factors as the United States growing strategic partnership with Pakistan, Nepal continued to feel the effect. From the 1970s onward, for the duration of the Cold War, Nepal was caught between the Indo-Soviet and Sino-American pressures.

Affirmations of an abiding convergence of US-Indian views on Nepal are bound to deepen concerns of Nepalese already unable to feel a partnership of equality with their southern neighbour. Yet on closer examination, the Washington-New Delhi convergence may not be as watertight as assumed. Although both Washington and New Delhi had declared the Nepalese Maoists terrorists and armed the Nepalese military to fight them, the disparate prisms of the US-led global war on terrorism and India's regional possessiveness produced views that had to be reconciled. Between 2002 and 2005, New Delhi and Washington seemed to be on the same page regarding the growing Maoist insurgency in Nepal. Yet Washington pressed the palace toward a military solution, while India had already established contacts with Maoist leaders to forestall a wider conflict. Despite its disenchantment with King Gyanendra, the United States was dubious of India's effort to mainstream the Maoists until the very end.

From the Chinese perspective, the United States used the Maoist insurgency to build its presence in Nepal as part of the wider post-9/11 global military build-up. Washington's stress on the identity of views with New Delhi on Nepal, in the Chinese view, was more of a calculated ploy to overcome Indian opposition to a greater American role. Kathmandu saw one of the biggest

American embassy build-ups in the post-9/11 era. President Barack Obama's administration, along with its public assertions of its intentions to chart an independent course on Nepal, sought greater funding for its embassy in Kathmandu. By allowing the Americans some leeway in Nepal, Beijing may have hoped to dilute Indian influence and chip away at the containment alliance. The Obama administration, too, played along by conferring on Beijing a stakeholder status in Nepal equivalent to what New Delhi had traditionally reserved for itself.

Even today, amid the clamour for a stronger US-Indian effort to contain a belligerent China, average Nepalese recognise the depth of India's ambivalence. For long, Washington and New Delhi denied the existence of an anti-Chinese element in their strategic partnership. In the era of COVID-19, such denials have become irrelevant. Long before the abolition of the Nepalese monarchy, China had begun appraising how the Indo-US trajectory would affect Nepal and calibrating its response. From the vast Chinese state commentary on the country's triangular relationship with India and the United States, there is considerable analysis on the constraints to the ability of the world's two largest democracies to work together everywhere. As a member of such diverse forums as the Shanghai Cooperation Organization, BRICS and the 'Quad', India may have become the world's largest swing country. Watching a confounded India address the attendant contradictions seems to have become the Chinese commentariat's favourite pastime. Each time Beijing praises the virtues of New Delhi's tradition of strategic autonomy, Indian analysts respond by highlighting the differences of the Tibet and Taiwan cards in terms of their value and viability. India can perhaps rely on the United States on the maritime front, but the risk of isolation along the Himalayas is as assured as the permafrost there. The mid-hills and southern plains of Nepal some latitudes below may not be too hospitable for comprehensive Indo-US engagement.

The relative strengths and weaknesses of China at any given point in history may have determined the level of its influence in Nepal, but Beijing has always remained a significant external variable. Mired in civil war, China could hardly entertain the beleaguered Ranas overtures as the British rulers prepared to leave the subcontinent. China's subsequent domestic preoccupations and involvement in the Korean War allowed India to speed up its political, economic and security ties with Nepal. In 1954, despite New Delhi's closeness to Beijing, Nehru had tried to dissuade the Nepalese leadership from establishing diplomatic relations with China. Eventually, he had given his assent to Nepal establishing such relations with China but asserted that Sino-Nepalese discussions were best conducted in Delhi, rather than Kathmandu or Beijing (Madan, 2020).

In 1956, the Indian government learned from Zhou Enlai that China and Nepal were thinking of signing a Panchsheel-like agreement. The Chinese premier also indicated that Nepal wanted China to establish a consulate-general in Kathmandu. Internally, Nehru objected to a Sino-Nepalese treaty, especially since it increased each country's presence in the other. He was concerned that Kathmandu had kept Delhi out of the loop on its interactions with China as well as the Soviet Union. Still, in September 1956, China and Nepal signed a trade and travel agreement and agreed to set up consulates general in the other country. Nepal also accepted economic aid and industrial equipment from China.

Ever since the Sino-Indian war of 1962, China has become an even more pivotal factor in Nepal-India relations. King Mahendra's eagerness to project Nepal's independent identity conformed to Nepalese misgivings over Indian motives as well as China's growing assertiveness. Beijing's decision to build closer ties with Kathmandu was rooted in its wider policy of building relations with non-Communist Asian countries to break out of its isolation resulting from the United States and United Nations embargo. China's increased participation in Nepal's economic development was part of its strategy to neutralise India's influence. Beijing's success in articulating as well as projecting a policy of non-interference, coupled with an infusion of unconditional aid, resonated with the aspirations of the Nepalese.

Some Indians suggest that since 1954 China and India have had an understanding on Nepal. India and China, this interpretation goes, would do nothing to undermine each other's vital interests beyond the Himalayas. According to this understanding, India has been hosting the Dalai Lama's government in exile without supporting its claims for independence or greater autonomy for Tibet. If there was such an arrangement on Nepal and it had survived the 1962 war, the Chinese gave little indication of its existence. Beijing's reluctance to fully support its ally, Pakistan, during the 1971 Indo-Pak war underscored Chinese limits in challenging India's regional supremacy. The creation of Bangladesh over Beijing's strong – yet largely rhetorical – opposition reinforced this reality. Yet China continued to maintain a consistent anti-Indian posture in Nepal. Until Mao Zedong's death in 1976, Radio Beijing and the New

China News Agency regularly referred to Indian interference in Nepalese internal affairs and accused New Delhi of pursuing expansionist policies in the kingdom. The moderates' ascension to political power in Beijing obscured such rhetoric, but not the recognition of that reality.

The Sino-Indian thaw inaugurated by Prime Minister Rajiv Gandhi's landmark visit to China in 1988 influenced the political events in Nepal. Clearly, Beijing was unwilling to intervene on Nepal's behalf during the 1989-1990 crisis, even though it had resulted directly from Chinese weapons sales to the kingdom. Reeling from international condemnation of the Tiananmen Square massacre amid the global onslaught on communism, Beijing's reluctance was understandable. At a news conference in Kathmandu, visiting Prime Minister Li Peng urged Nepal to settle its differences with India.

Although Beijing voiced concern over growing Indian influence in Nepal following the restoration of multiparty democracy, publicly it seemed to accede to Nepal's traditional links with its southern neighbour. When the CPN-UML gained power in 1994, Indian analysts noted how China had worked to assure India it would not take advantage of that situation. Even under its first communist government, Nepal still maintained an India-centric approach.

The outbreak of the Maoist insurgency two years later raised apprehensions in China. For the Chinese, the ease with which the Nepalese rebels could use Indian territory to mount a spree of death and destruction that defamed their Great Helmsman was alarming enough. The attempt by some in India and the West to blame China for sponsoring the Nepalese insurgency added to the distrust. George Fernandes' foray into Tibet via Nepal under the auspices of the independence movement, before his assertion as defence minister that India had conducted its 1998 nuclear tests to counter the threat from China, forced Beijing to reconsider the limits of its tolerance of the Kathmandu-New Delhi bonhomie. The escape of the Karmapa Lama, the third-ranking spiritual leader in Tibet, to India through Nepal in 2000 drew the kingdom into the vortex of insecurity. The sudden acceleration of high-level political and security contacts between Kathmandu and Beijing during the last year of King Birendra's reign did not occur in a vacuum.

China's palpable reluctance to come out in stronger support of King Gyanendra's direct rule was seen at the time as an indicator of the limits to which Beijing could diverge from New Delhi. In retrospect, it was the outcome of a far shrewder calculation aimed at covering any eventuality. China seems to have calibrated the course correction it expected from Nepal and now reached the point where it shapes events, not merely reacting to them.

Chinese acquiescence in India's primacy in Nepal – if that is a correct characterisation of Beijing's stand even when it professes it – would operate within the context of China's interests. Yet Indian commentators and analysts have taken gleeful pride at instances where they saw Beijing discarding Kathmandu. In far subdued tones, however, Chinese analysts refused to acknowledge that phases of pullback represented a conscious decision by Beijing to recognise Indian paramountcy in Nepal. The logical extension of that contention would be a resumption of Chinese rivalry with India for influence in Nepal and wider South Asia when circumstances became more propitious for Beijing (Garver, 2001).

The Nepalese recognise that this complicated relationship between two giants with divergent political systems and contending global ambitions must make prudent allowances for cooperation, competition and confrontation. China's arrival in South Asia has altered the region's centre of gravity – a shift that will have lasting reverberations on Nepal and its ties with India. The Nepalese realise that while a stronger Chinese presence may balance India, it may also raise the risk of heightened interference from powers other than these two growing and assertive neighbours. There is recognition of Nepal's need to develop a consensus on foreign policy to avoid such interference. However, a major obstacle is the deeply partisan bickering among the different political forces. True, such interference occurs because Nepalese politicians and policymakers seek external assistance for partisan, factional, and personal advantage. But where would they be without the eager helpers?

China has clear motivations to push its strategic and economic interests in South Asia. These include stabilising its Tibetan and Xinjiang periphery, entering the potentially large South Asian market, expanding its outreach in the Indian Ocean to resolve the 'Malacca Dilemma' and countering the adversarial influence of the United States and India in these countries. The smaller South Asian states support China's BRI despite India's opposition to the enterprise. Through Nepal, China is building a strategic Himalayan corridor for development (Muni, 2020). From New Delhi's standpoint, this Chinese push encroaches on India's vital strategic space in the neighbourhood. New Delhi feels China's forceful presence in South Asia would keep India constrained in its role in Asia and threaten its internal stability and territorial security.

Narendra Modi's 'Neighbourhood First' policy, which followed China's announcement of the BRI, refocused India's attention away from a foreign policy preoccupied with Pakistan and major power dynamics. However, the new policy faltered in Nepal the following year through New Delhi's rough diplomatic intervention in the constitutional process and its subsequent informal economic blockade. The Modi government continues to pursue the policy as catalyst and corrective. The Indian leadership has been making more frequent high-level visits to neighbouring countries and maintains regular contacts with the ruling and opposition sides. Indian leaders are reaching out more actively to the average citizens there by boosting cultural and civilisation links. New Delhi has been speeding up the pace of bilateral projects and extends prompt and massive support for disaster relief. During the COVID-19 pandemic, it tried to revive SAARC and continues to provide medicines and volunteers to its neighbours.

Coupled with India's realisation of its inability to compete with China in financial terms is the recognition that the rivalry in South Asia will persist. What has thus emerged is a two-pronged approach of bandwagoning with other powers sceptical of China's motives and intentions, while seeking to draw Beijing into constructive engagement through informal bilateral summits and official multilateral forums.

Still, that balance is not as tenable as it once might have been. In the initial years, Beijing viewed New Delhi's understanding of the Indo-Pacific Strategy in geographic rather than strategic dimensions. Chinese analysts seem to have revised their assessment based on recent developments. They see India strengthening cooperation with the United States in the Indian Ocean and playing a growing role in setting the agenda for maritime cooperation. Beijing notes an acceleration of efforts to institutionalise the 'Quad' precisely when New Delhi has been taking palpable steps towards a partial decoupling from China (Ren and Wu, 2020). Chinese analysts see the likelihood of relations with India encompassing both competitive cooperation and cooperative competition with the particular attributes varying with the context and circumstances of the moment.

As benign as that formulation may sound in its general articulation, it intensifies Nepal's predicaments. One challenge in this wider context is best illustrated by the MCC compact. India, a party to the accord while recognising that the MCC is a central part of the US Indo-Pacific Strategy, has maintained a low profile in the controversy raging inside Nepal. Despite its public reticence, Beijing's underlying opposition to the MCC in Nepal has been responsible for its increasingly audacious interventions in the internal affairs of the ruling party. It becomes fair to ask how much New Delhi may be contributing to the Chinese pressures emanating from Nepal it so decries.

Despite recognising that India facilitated the SPA-Maoist alliance out of self-interest, few Nepalese dispute that a peace process could have been put in place without New Delhi's sustained involvement. Some early signs were encouraging. India had signalled a readiness to build a new partnership. By agreeing to a United Nations role in the peace process, India had given up some of its traditional monopoly in Nepal. The United Nations Security Council resolution establishing the peace mission in Nepal had been careful to emphasise its limited political focus. The resolution was candid in its acknowledgement of the special roles of India and that of China, which had shed its own reservations on a UN role in Nepal. If New Delhi's change marked a grudging acceptance of the growth of American, Chinese and Western European influence in Nepal, perhaps the Nepalese were justified in hoping to exercise their sovereign choices with greater independence.

During his visit to Kathmandu in December 2006, Foreign Secretary Shiv Shankar Menon affirmed India's willingness to review the 1950 Treaty in the most candid language any Indian official had so far used. The Nepalese had sought a loosening of political ties, sacrificing none of the economic benefits. Most Nepalese might not know that the Nepalese rupee's dollar exchange rate still is stable because it is actually pegged to the Indian rupee via the open border. But they do feel it. The clamour for a revision of the treaty results from the imbalance between the political loss and economic gain. At least New Delhi conceded it as a genuine demand. As successive governments continue to reiterate the pledge with no action, many Nepalese wonder how much of the change is for real. India's continued refusal to accept something as benign as the Eminent Persons Group report for its non-binding recommendations has raised serious questions. Could the much-heralded new beginning be New Delhi's way of deflecting criticism of its interventionism and pursuing other modes of maintaining control? Kathmandu may have taken its time to ponder. Beijing apparently did not miss a beat.

IN THE END, it is all in the mind. Given the topographical similarities and contiguity, India sees Nepal as part of its northern security system. It feels vulnerable in case external powers expanded their presence on Nepalese territory beyond the normal diplomatic activity. New Delhi, therefore, expects Kathmandu to remain sensitive to its security concerns. Nepal sees this expectation as an infringement on its sovereignty and independence.

At one level, Indians are not wrong to wonder whether Nepal is doing China's bidding. After all, the new Nepalese map has left out the Susta sector, the other element of the territorial dispute. If Prime Minister Oli's claim that Lord Ram was born in Nepal sounded like an attempt to break Nepal's civilisational relationship with India, perhaps it is because Indians have not forgotten how stung they were by Zhou Enlai's assertion in the 1950s that China had blood relations with Nepal. But times have changed in all three countries.

Given the subsequent turn of events in the region from India's standpoint, perhaps Sardar Vallabh Bhai Patel turned out to be more prophetic than he was at the time he sought Nepal's inclusion in the Indian Union. Yet in Nehru's view, bilateral treaties of friendship and peace with the three northern Himalayan kingdoms – Bhutan, Nepal and Sikkim – and an offer of a no-war pact to Pakistan was enough to deal with South Asia (Pande, 2020) freeing him to seek prominence on the Asian and global stage. No handwringing can change the fact that Nepal has remained an independent nation ever since.

The 1950 Treaty of Peace and Friendship between Nehru's ambassador and the absolute ruler of a tottering oligarchy may have been one way India thought it could handle the three disparate Himalayan states. That Nepal did not go the way of Sikkim (annexation) or Bhutan (protectorate) is as much a fact as is the reality that India-Nepal relations are regulated by the

1950 Treaty. The two countries agreed to grant each other's citizens national treatment in all matters, including taking up jobs, doing business and owning property. This was ensured through an open border and the free circulation of Indian currency in Nepal. Evidently, the benefits were obviously more for Nepal, whose citizens could take advantage of India's big market and higher level of development. In practice, the Indians could not get reciprocal benefits because of the same asymmetries. As it resembled the 1923 Nepal-Britain Treaty, the 1950 Treaty did not materially change the existing situation. Nor was there any viable alternative before either side, given the absence of any natural geographical boundaries or traditional of regulating the India–Nepal border (Sikri, 2009).

Equally important is the fact that Nepal came to the treaty table intending to assert and preserve its status as a sovereign nation. If Nehru's notion of security expressed through the 1950 Treaty had resonance for Nepal, it was to the extent of ensuring an independent Nepal did not threaten India's interests. It may be entirely fortuitous that the new treaty triggered a chain of events that would culminate in the grand Delhi Compromise. Still, the parties and palace that displaced the Ranas adhered to Nepal's original expectation from the treaty. Only nine years later, when Nepal was under an elected government, would the reciprocity the Indians sought become public knowledge, when New Delhi revealed the confidential exchange of side letters to the treaty.

Those letters obliged Nepal to depend on India for its security. In case of any threat to the security of the other by a foreign aggressor, the two governments would consult with each other and devise effective countermeasures. Nepal agreed that it would not import arms, ammunition and other military equipment except with India's consent. Yet when Nepal and India agreed to joint manning of posts on the Nepal–Tibet border and set up an Indian Military Mission in Nepal, they did so when Nepal feared a Chinese threat, particularly after the Chinese occupation of Tibet. These steps were not Kathmandu's confirmation of India's invocation of any right to control Nepal's political and economic life.

The security aspects lost their relevance as Nepal established diplomatic ties with China and concluded their boundary agreement, Nepal's pursuit of a foreign policy intended to assert its independent identity no longer automatically provided India a second vote at the United Nations General Assembly. A landlocked country dependent on transit through India for trade with third countries went on to find new opportunities for economic diversification. Thus, adhering to international law, it considered transit to be a right but trade a matter of convenience.

Every time Nepal sought a review, India pointed to the provision for unilateral termination on a year's notice. It was only after democratically elected leaders in the 1990s began pressing the case that New Delhi agreed to discuss the matter. Yet even some of the same Indians who acknowledge how the Indian government and public have never shown adequate sensitivity to Nepalese pride in their sovereignty and independence have difficulty in seeing Kathmandu's assertion of its independence as more than skilful leveraging of its geographical contiguity with China. During the latest border dispute, many Indian experts and analysts have placed much faith in how the unique people-to-people relations would see the two countries through this crisis. While urging India to do everything it should to nurture the invaluable asset it has in the goodwill of the Nepalese people, some in this fraternity still counsel India to reject the Nepalese state's ill-conceived territorial claims.

Prime Minister Narendra Modi's pledge in 2014 to see a revision done during his tenure and invitation to Nepal to present proposals was the clearest articulation of India's change of heart. Yet Modi still has had the time to receive the report prepared by the bilateral Eminent Persons Group in 2018. How much are pledges worth if a set of nonbinding recommendations agreed together cannot merit sufficient official attention in New Delhi?

A leading Chinese expert on South Asia contends that India itself was prompting Beijing to reassess its policy in the region (Zhao, 2010). Arguing that New Delhi failed to address the 'strategic autonomy' of other South Asian nations, he described the resultant discordance as a threat to Chinese interests. If India is anxious to lead South Asia by virtue of its size and strength, he contended, then it must only do so with the consent of its smaller neighbours. As to Nepal, short of annexing the country and assuming the associated costs, India can do little but reconcile itself to the fact that it is an independent nation. Catchphrases like 'special relations' or 'roti-beti' cannot help because they have become terms of estrangement. Just as India cannot apologise for being big, Nepal must not be expected to pay the price of being small and sandwiched between two giants that distrust each other. Nepal's grievances with China might not seem as serious as those with India, but they do exist. Beijing has maintained relative silence on the substance of the

India-Nepal border dispute, preferring to club it together with China's general support for Nepalese sovereignty. Yet China has not hesitated to send subtle reminders that the Kalapani question is quite identical to one concerning Doklam.

Nepal recognises that most pledges from China to ease the country's dependence on India foresee the long term. Moreover, little of tangible consequence has even begun, a fact that has the potential to raise public impatience. Greater exposure to Chinese business tactics, the darker side of growing interactions such as crime, and the general Chinese perceptions of themselves and their place in the world risk bringing more Nepalese discontent to the fore. Dismissing Nepalese grievances with India as Chinese-instigated ploys could present New Delhi with stricter challenges from Beijing from Nepal. This assertion stems not from Nepalese arrogance but from anguish over the additional pain that might be inflicted upon the country.

So, instead of obsessing over why the Nepalese see China the way they do, India might want to delve deeper into how China sees Nepal. Although it might not advertise it, Beijing sees Tibet and Nepal as part of its integrated 'peripheral policy'. Nepal's northern border is an easy gateway to the Tibet Autonomous Region. China worries that political instability in Nepal could lead to enhanced anti-Chinese activities in Nepal. Every time India is tempted to wave the Tibet card to China, it is enough to wobble Nepal.

Although Beijing considers the situation in the Tibetan region more stable, it expects the region to continue to be a core factor in relations with Kathmandu. With the three external powers most active on the Tibet issue – India, the United States and the European Union – increasingly involved in Nepal's peace process, Beijing's concerns about renewed potential for destabilisation from that volatile frontier have grown. The inevitable passing of the Fourteenth Dalai Lama and ensuing succession politics are certain to energise an increasingly restless exile community in Nepal and those living across the porous border in India.

The Chinese passed regulations in 2007 that, in effect, ensured their final say in the choice of the new Dalai Lama. Tenzin Gyatso, who in March 2011 announced his retirement from active day-to-day leadership, has said in the past that he might break tradition and name a successor and that his successor might not even be reincarnated inside Tibet. To forestall potential unrest inside Tibet, Beijing had begun adopting multi-pronged measures. Substantial levels of aid have been pledged for the estimated 6.5 million Tibetans living in what Beijing has designated as the Tibet Autonomous Region as well as the neighbouring provinces of Sichuan, Gansu and Qinghai.

For long, many Indians have believed that a resolution of the Tibet issue held the key to a durable settlement of their disputes with China. Now hardliners in India are becoming more forthright in their assertion that New Delhi should exploit what they consider China's Achilles heel. To secure progress on the border question or on Kashmir, they feel India should remind the Chinese that they could raise the cost in Tibet.

Considering China's growing sensitivities ahead of an impending vicious struggle over the Dalai Lama succession issue, Beijing is likely to see India's use of the 'Tibet card' as a dangerous escalation. The unprecedented media publicity given to the participation of the Special Frontier Forces – an elite paratrooper unit drawn mainly from India's Tibetan exile community – alongside regular Indian army units in a key battle has raised the stakes considerably (Ramachandran, 2020). A new security crisis in Tibet would create a substantial flow of refugees into Nepal, increasing its geostrategic vulnerabilities.

The Chinese have moved beyond Tibet in their engagement with Nepal, at least in the traditional sense. There is new recognition in China that, given its border disputes with India and absence of diplomatic relations with Bhutan, only Nepal could provide it physical connectivity to South Asia (Hu Shisheng, 2015). Beijing has divided South Asia into western (Afghanistan and Pakistan) and eastern (India at the centre) components and sees Nepal the most viable bridge to the latter. Expressions of such benign motives are not going to impress India, which has long seen Chinese trans-Himalayan ambitions as growing from a desire to keep a check on India's rising capabilities.

More broadly, however, it would be critical to juxtapose the future with the past to explore where Nepal may lie amid the contours of an emerging Sino-centric world. Most analysts concede that the visible elements of China's recent assertiveness can be interpreted in various ways. Still, they note striking similarities between the ancient tribute system and the way Beijing currently engages with parts of the outside world (Rolland, 2020). These moves do not indicate a coherent model enlivening every aspect of China's diplomatic practice. But this may also be because the tribute system, while a manifestation of Confucian norms of hierarchy, was, in the words of John K. Fairbank, a "repertoire of means available to the rulers of the

Chinese empire in their relations with non-Chinese…along a spectrum that runs from one extreme of military conquest and administrative assimilation to another extreme of complete nonintercourse and avoidance of contact" (Fairbank, 1968).

Today, under the Xi Jinping Thought on Socialism with Chinese Characteristics for a New Era, the strands of tianxia (everything under heaven) appear interwoven with a modern Marxist-Leninist power structure, organisation, and ideological system (Rolland, 2020). In that case, it becomes important to remember that Nepal was the last tributary to the Qing Dynasty. For a country with a prodigiously long memory and a pragmatic sense of historical continuity, the implications are immense for China. Knowing that, Mao Zedong's 'five-fingers and a palm' analogy would cease to oscillate between evoking distress and derision in New Delhi and begin encouraging an understanding of the ceaseless churning that goes on in Beijing.

At the practical level, a deeper understanding could even foster some creative thinking by India and China. Terms like 'trilateral cooperation', 'corridor' and 'bridge' are anathema to New Delhi in the context of China, Nepal and India. Frustrated, some Chinese analysts have called for Beijing and Kathmandu to move ahead with trans-Himalayan development, with or without New Delhi (Hu Shisheng, 2017). China and India have always shared competing national interests in and over Nepal. Experience has taught Kathmandu it may be largely irrelevant if China and India are 'good' to Nepal without also being good to each other (Koirala, 2011). Given their simultaneous rise and great power aspirations, that rivalry is likely to intensify.

King Birendra's 1975 Zone of Peace proposal – which over

the next decade and a half won the support of 116 countries – envisioned 'institutionalising peace in the region' to safeguard Nepal's independence and territorial integrity through the unpredictable vicissitudes of history and time. India's strong and consistent opposition was enough for the drafters of the 1990 Constitution to discard it. What has endured is the reality of Nepal's enormously geostrategic location between India and China, which have a proven history of military conflicts (Josse, 2020).

Theoretically, the 2+1 dialogue mechanism would help India and China narrow their mutual suspicions sufficiently to spur Nepal's development. Practically, though, it would be a non-starter. Whether relations with Beijing are in thaw or tense, India is no mood to further diminish Nepal's status as its exclusive zone of influence. A more financially and diplomatically energised China would take a more sweeping world view to developing mutually beneficial bilateral relations with Nepal. In such a situation, Nepal's own perplexity becomes understandable.

The concept first emerged during the April 2018 Xi-Modi informal summit in Wuhan, convened against the backdrop of the Doklam standoff. China proposed the model as a way of minimising conflict with India over smaller South Asian states. During Prime Minister Oli's visit to China in June, Xi briefly shared his discussions with Modi on the concept. The Chinese and Indian leaders discussed the 2+1 mechanism during their second informal summit in Mamallapuram. Xi's decision to fly to Nepal from India – as opposed to travelling from China – may have reflected Beijing's desire to inaugurate this concept (Bhattarai, 2019).

During talks in Kathmandu, Xi shared the proposal with

Nepalese leaders. Rejecting it, Oli was said to have explained to Xi Nepal's preference for trilateral cooperation. Oli later explained that partnerships needed to be based on equality. Many Nepalese experts began stressing that the 2+1 approach undermined Nepal's ability to deal independently with its neighbours on important projects. The 2+1 mechanism required Nepalese concurrence with what China and India could agree on. That way the economic dimensions of cooperation would be made subservient to the security considerations of Nepal's two neighbours. China's continued insistence is believed to have partly contributed to Oli's renewed eagerness to secure parliamentary endorsement of the MCC compact with the United States. Just as the onus fell on Nepal to amplify its preference, COVID-19 blended the underlying contradictions of the Sino-Indian relationship into the border conflict. New Delhi was likely to torpedo either model even before relations with Beijing nosedived. China had made sufficient economic, social and diplomatic investments allowing it to become more active and assertive in Nepal.

Yet the core challenge remains unchanged: All three countries must devise a way to ensure that Nepal does not continue to be drawn into the Sino-Indian vortex only to be denigrated as a source of their conflict.

Glossary

AISC – Army Integration Special Committee: Headed by the Prime Minister, the AISC was set up in October 2008 for the supervision, integration and rehabilitation of the Maoist army combatants.

Asian-African Conference: Summit in Indonesia in April 2005 on the sidelines of which King Gyanendra and Prime Minister Manmohan Singh held their first talks after the royal takeover.

Bhutanese refugees: Over 100,000 Nepali-speaking Bhutanese who fled their homeland in the early 1990 citing persecution, lodged in camps in eastern Nepal.

BIMSTEC – Bay of Bengal Initiative for Multi-Sectoral Technical and Economic Cooperation: An international organisation of seven nations of South Asia and Southeast Asia based in Dhaka, Bangladesh.

BJP – Bharatiya Janata Party: Hindu nationalist party of India with close ties with the Nepalese monarchy.

Boao Forum for Asia: A China-based non-governmental, not-for-profit international organisation modelled after the World Economic Forum in Davos, Switzerland.

BRI – Belt and Road Initiative: An ambitious Chinese programme to connect Asia with Africa and Europe via land and maritime networks along six corridors with the aim of improving regional integration, increasing trade and stimulating economic growth.

BRICS – A group composed by the five major emerging countries - Brazil, Russia, India, China and South Africa.

CA – Constituent Assembly: A unicameral body of 601 members elected in April 2008 to draft Nepal's new Constitution. The body served from May 28, 2008 to May 28, 2012, when it was dissolved failing to write the Constitution. A second Constituent Assembly, elected in 2013, promulgated the Constitution in 2015. It later converted to the Legislature Parliament whose term ended on October 14, 2017.

CCP – Chinese Communist Party:

'China Card': Indian term for Nepal's purported propensity to assert its closeness with China to extract concessions from New Delhi.

CIA – Central Intelligence Agency of the United States.

CPA – Comprehensive Peace Accord: November 2006 agreement between the Nepalese government and Maoist rebels formally ending a decade-long insurgency that claimed over 17,000 lives.

CPM – Communist Party of India-Marxist: Indian communist organisation that played a leading role in facilitating the November 2005 alliance of Nepalese opposition parties and Maoist rebels against King Gyanendra's direct rule.

CPN-M – CPN-Maoist: Founded on 24 November 2014 and currently led by General Secretary Netra Bikram Chand (commonly known as 'Biplab'). The party – holding the name of the group that waged a decade-long people's war – was created after its founders accused Pushpa Kamal Dahal, Baburam Bhattarai and Mohan Baidya 'Kiran' of abandoning the revolution.

CPN-MC – Communist Party of Nepal-Maoist Centre: A communist party that existed from 1994 to 2018. The party led three governments, from 2008 to 2009 and from 2016 to 2017 under Pushpa Kamal Dahal and from 2013 to 2015 under Baburam Bhattarai. The party was previously known as the Communist Party of Nepal-Maoist until 2009 and as the Unified Communist Party of Nepal-Maoist until 2016.

CPN-UML – Communist Party of Nepal-Unified Marxist-Leninist: One of the two major communist parties in Nepal from 1991 to 2018, the CPN-UML was formed in January 1991 with the unification of the Communist Party of Nepal-Marxist and the Communist Party of Nepal-Marxist-Leninist. The CPN-UML led four governments: from 1994 to 1995 under Man Mohan Adhikari; from 2009 to 2011 under Madhav Kumar Nepal; in 2011 under Jhal Nath Khanal, and from 2015 to 2016 under KP Sharma Oli. The party dissolved on May 17, 2018 to make way for the Nepal Communist Party in a merger with the Communist Party of Nepal-Maoist Centre.

Cultural Revolution: A struggle for power from 1966 to 1976 within the Communist Party of China that manifested in wide-scale social, political, and economic chaos, which grew to include large sections of Chinese society and eventually brought the entire country to the brink of civil war.

Delhi Compromise: Tripartite agreement between King Tribhuvan, the Ranas and the Nepali Congress mediated by Prime Minister Jawaharlal Nehru in 1951 that ushered in an era of multiparty politics under a constitutional monarchy in Nepal.

East India Company: An early joint-stock company granted an English Royal Charter with the intention of favouring trade privileges in India. The Royal Charter effectively gave the Company a monopoly on all trade in the East Indies. The Company transformed from a commercial trading venture to one that virtually ruled India as it acquired auxiliary governmental and military functions, until its dissolution following the Indian Mutiny of 1857.

EPG – Eminent Persons Group: Consisting of relevant experts from India and Nepal, the EPG was formed in early 2016 to review all the bilateral treaties and agreements between the two countries, including the controversial 1950 Treaty of Peace and Friendship.

EU – European Union

Gorakhpur: One of the Indian cities closest to the border with Nepal.

Gorkha: A small kingdom in western Nepal where the Shah dynasty originated.

Greater Nepal: The combined territory of present-day Nepal and lands the kingdom was forced to cede to the British after the 1814-1816 war.

Gurkhas: Nepalese hillspeople known for their fighting prowess recruited by the British and Indian armies.

HLPC – High Level Political Committee: A cross-party mechanism responsible for settling disputed issues related to peace and Constitution drafting process.

House of Representatives: Lower house of the Nepalese parliament directly elected by the people.

Human Rights Watch: New York based organisation that was among the leading critics of King Gyanendra's government.

Janakpur: Seat of the ancient Mithila kingdom of Janak, father of Lord Ram's consort, Sita, today it is a major city in the Nepalese plains.

Jhapa: District in the eastern Nepalese plains and former hotbed of radical communism.

Kalapani: A 35 square kilometre area on Nepal's western border which Kathmandu insists India unlawfully occupies and must vacate.

Kapilvastu: District in southwestern Nepal where the Buddha was born.

Kathmandu Valley: The valley containing the three ancient kingdoms of Kantipur, Patan and Bhadgaon.

Kerung: One of the two major mountain passes into Tibet.

Kosi River: One of the major Nepalese rivers, in the eastern part of the country, flowing into India.

Kosi Treaty: A 1954 agreement between Nepal and India on jointly harnessing the waters of the Kosi, which many Nepalese consider highly unfavourable to their country.

Kuti: One of the two major mountain passes into Tibet.

Lhasa: Capital city of Tibet.

Lipulekh: A Himalayan pass on the border between India's Uttarakhand state and the Tibet region of China, near their trijunction with Nepal. Nepal has ongoing claims to the southern side of the pass, called Kalapani territory, which is controlled by India.

Limpiyadhura: A Himalayan pass and area where Nepal claims is the origin of the Mahakali River – its western boundary under the Sugauli Treaty of 1816 with British India. It incorporated the area, together with the other adjoining Indian-occupied territories of Lipulekh and Kalapani in a new political map in 2020.

MJF – Madhesi Janadhikar Forum: An organisation spearheading a movement to end what it calls discrimination against Nepalese native to the southern plains.

MJF-D – Madhesi Janadhikar Forum-Democratic (Loktantrik in Nepali), party formed by Bijay Kumar Gachhadar when he and other members split from the original MJF in 2009.

MCC – Millennium Challenge Corporation: Also refers to the compact between the US Millennium Challenge Corporation and the Nepalese government designed to increase the availability of electricity and lower the cost of transportation in Nepal.

Maoist insurgency: Decade-long insurgency that began in 1996 to overthrow Nepal's monarchy and parliamentary democracy, claiming over 17,000 lives.

NA - Nepal Army, until 2006 the Royal Nepal Army.

Narayanhity Massacre: June 1, 2001 attack in which Crown Prince Dipendra opened fire on King Birendra, Queen Aishwarya, his siblings and other royal relatives before turning the gun on himself. Many Nepalese dispute the official version.

Narayanhity Royal Palace: Residence and offices of the Nepalese monarch and his family.

NC - Nepali Congress: Nepali Congress: Formed in 1950 in Calcutta with the merger of the Nepali National Congress and the Nepali Democratic Congress, it is the country's largest democratic political party.
NCP – Nepal Communist Party: The ruling political party in Nepal founded on May 17, 2018 from the unification of two leftist parties, Communist Party of Nepal-Unified Marxist-Leninist and

Communist Party of Nepal-Maoist Centre.

NEFIN – Nepal Federation of Indigenous Nationalities: Alliance of groups representing indigenous communities of Nepal.

Naxalites: Another name for Indian Maoists in reference to the Naxalbari insurrection by radical Maoists in West Bengal in 1967.

NSP – Nepal Sadbhavana Party: Terai-based party a faction of which is part of the ruling coalition.

OBOR – One Belt One Road: The predecessor to China's Belt and Road Initiative.

Panchashila: Five principles of peaceful coexistence among nations, has its root in Buddhism.

Panchayat system: Partyless system King Mahendra formally introduced two years after ousting Nepal's first elected government and abolishing the parliamentary system in 1960.

Pashupatinath: The most important Hindu pilgrim centre of Nepal.

PLA – People's Liberation Army: The army of the Maoist party, which fought the state for ten
years, now disbanded.

Qing Empire: Realm of the last ruling dynasty of China from 1644 to 1911.

Rana Regime: 104-year-old system in which hereditary premiers exercised total power, reducing monarchs to virtual prisoners, which ended with the 1951 Delhi Compromise.

RAW – Research and Analysis Wing: India's external intelligence agency.

RNA – Royal Nepalese Army: The official designation of the country's military until the new democratic government removed the royal prefix.

RPP – Rastriya Prajatantra Party: An amalgamation of parties formed by workers of the partyless Panchayat system after the restoration of multiparty democracy in 1990. Its modern version includes factions led by Kamal Thapa, Pashupati Shamsher Rana and Prakash Chandra Lohani, who serve as co-chairs.

RPP-N – Rastriya Prajatantra Party-Nepal: Between 2006 and 2016, it was the only political party that advocated a return to the monarchy and reinstatement of the Hindu state. Led by Kamal Thapa, it came a distant fourth in the 2013 election and gained significant leverage in the formation of coalitions. It united with other factions in 2016 to become the RPP.

SAARC – The South Asian Association for Regional Cooperation: formed in 1985.

SPA – Seven Party Alliance: A group of seven mainstream opposition parties formed to oppose King Gyanendra's takeover in 2005, which later joined hands with the Maoists to oust the royal regime.

Singha Darbar: The sprawling palace complex Chandra Shamsher Rana built, which now houses the government secretariat.

Special Relations: India's characterisation of its relations with Nepal, which is resented by many Nepalese.

Susta: Border settlement, close to the birthplace of Lord Buddha, which Nepal has long accused India of encroaching.

Syabrubesi-Rasuwagadi Road: A proposed second road linking Nepal with China.

Tanakpur Project: An Indian dam project on the Mahakali River part of which took up Nepalese territory following, it turned out, a secret understanding in 1991 with the government of Prime Minister Girija Prasad Koirala. The controversy snowballed into a major political issue, leading to the collapse of his government three years later.

TAR – Tibet Autonomous Region

Terai: The fertile strip of plains on Nepal's southern border with India.

Tiananmen Square massacre: The crushing of pro-democracy protests in the heart of Beijing in 1989, in which thousands of Chinese students were believed to have been killed by soldiers.
TMLP – Tarai Madhes Loktantrik Party: Member of the Madhesi Morcha, led by Mahanta Thakur, it is one of the parties formed when the Congress lost its Madhesi leadership to the Madhes movement in 2007.

Treaty of Perpetual Peace and Friendship: A 1923 treaty under which Britain confirmed the independence of Nepal and its special relationship with British India.

Treaty, Indo-Soviet: 1971 agreement seen by many as having placed India firmly in the Soviet camp.

Treaty, 1950: Peace and friendship between India and Nepal which many Nepalese continue to view as highly unfavourable to their country.

Treaty, Mahakali: Nepal-India treaty signed in 1996 concerning the integrated development of the Mahakali river including Sarada Barrage, Tanakpur Barrage and Pancheshwar Project.

Treaty, Sugauli: Treaty signed after the 1814-16 Anglo-Nepalese War under which Nepal was forced to cede part of its territories, limiting the country to within its current geographical boundaries.

UCPN-M – United Communist Party of Nepal-Maoist: Commonly called 'Maoists', which officially changed its name from Communist Party of Nepal-Maoist in January 2009. From 1996-2006, it waged a war, called the "People's War" by the party, against the state. The party split in 2012, and the splinters are named variations of Communist Party of Nepal-Maoist. On May 17, 2018 it merged with the Communist Party of Nepal-Unified Marxist-Leninist to become the ruling Nepal Communist Party.

UMDF – United Madhesi Democratic Front a political coalition of three Madhes-based political parties: Sadbhavana Party Tarai-

Madhes Loktantrik Party Madhesi Janadhikar Forum, Nepal.

UNIDO – United Nations Industrial Development Organisation:

UNMIN – United Nations Mission in Nepal: Special political mission created by the United Nations Security Council in 2007 to monitor the disarmament of Maoist rebels and the preparations for Constituent Assembly elections. It was in existence until 2011.

UPA – United Progressive Alliance: The Congress-led ruling alliance in New Delhi from 2004 to 2014.

YCL – Young Communist League: Youth wing of Nepal's former Maoist rebels.

ZOP – Zone of Peace Proposal: Made by King Birendra in 1975, which India considered specifically targeted against itself, the democratic government of 1990 withdrew it.

A Chronology of Key Events

1768	Gorkha ruler Prithvi Narayan Shah conquers Kathmandu and lays foundations for unified kingdom.
1792	Nepalese expansion halted by defeat at hands of Chinese in Tibet.
1814-16	Anglo-Nepalese War; culminates in treaty which establishes Nepal's current boundaries.
1846	Nepal falls under sway of hereditary chief ministers known as Ranas, who dominate the monarchy and cut off country from outside world.
1923	Treaty with Britain affirms Nepal's sovereignty.
1950	Anti-Rana forces based in India form alliance with monarch.

1951	End of Rana rule. Sovereignty of crown restored and anti-Rana rebels in Nepalese Congress Party form government.
1953	New Zealander Edmund Hillary and Nepal's Sherpa Tenzing Norgay become the first climbers to reach the summit of Mount Everest.
1955	Nepal joins the United Nations.
1955	King Tribhuvan dies, King Mahendra ascends throne.
1959	Multi-party constitution adopted.
1960	King Mahendra seizes control and suspends parliament, constitution and party politicsafter Nepali Congress wins elections with B. P. Koirala as premier.
1962	New constitution provides for non-party system of councils known as 'panchayat' under which king exercises sole power. First elections to Rastriya Panchayat held in 1963.
1972	King Mahendra dies, succeeded by Birendra.
1980	Constitutional referendum follows agitation for reform. Small majority favours keeping existing panchayat system. King agrees to allow direct elections to national assembly - but on a

	non-party basis.
1985	Nepali Congress begins civil disobedience campaign for restoration of multi-party system.
1986	New elections boycotted by the Nepali Congress.
1989	Trade and transit dispute with India leads to border blockade by Delhi resulting in worsening economic situation.
1990 February	Pro-democracy agitation coordinated by Nepali Congress and communist groups. Street protests suppressed by security forces resulting in deaths and mass arrests.
1990 April	King Birendra eventually bows to pressure; repeals Panchayat constitution; appoints Krishna Prasad Bhattarai interim Prime Minister.
1990 November	Constitution of the Kingdom of Nepal 1990 promulgated.
1991 May	Nepali Congress wins first democratic elections. Girija Prasad Koirala becomes prime minister.
1992 April	First local elections held; Nepali Congress emerges strongest.
1994 July	Koirala's government defeated in no-confidence

	motion; parliament dissolved.
1994 November	New elections lead to formation of CPN-UML government. Man Mohan Adhikari appointed Prime Minister of minority government.
1995 September	Man Mohan Adhikari government defeated in no-confidence motion; Sher Bahadur Deuba of the Nepali Congress assumes premiership.
1996 February	CPN-Maoist declare 'people's war'.
1997 March	Prime Minister Sher Bahadur Deuba loses no-confidence vote, ushering in period of increased political instability, with frequent changes of prime minister.
1997 September	Second local elections held; CPN-UML emerges strongest.
1999 May	Second general elections held; Nepali Congress wins majority; Krishna Prasad Bhattarai appointed Prime Minister.
2000 May	Girija Prasad Koirala replaces Bhattarai as Prime Minister.
2001 June	Crown Prince Dipendra kills King Birendra, Queen Aishwarya and several members of the royal family, before shooting himself. Birendra's brother, Gyanendra is crowned king.

2001 July | Maoist rebels step up campaign of violence. Prime Minister Girija Prasad Koirala quits over the violence; succeeded by Sher Bahadur Deuba.

2001 November | Maoists end four-month old truce with government, declare peace talks with government failed. Launch coordinated attacks on army and police posts. State of emergency declared. King Gyanendra orders army to crush the Maoist rebels. Many hundreds are killed in rebel and government operations in the following months.

2002 May | Parliament dissolved, fresh elections called amid political confrontation over extending the state of emergency. Sher Bahadur Deuba heads interim government, renews emergency. Nepali Congress splits.

2002 October | Deuba recommends postponement of parliamentary elections; King Gyanendra dismisses Deuba; appoints Lokendra Bahadur Chand Prime Minister.

2003 January | Rebels, government declare ceasefire.

2003 August | Rebels pull out of peace talks with government and end seven-month truce. The following months see resurgence of violence and frequent

	clashes between students/activists and police.
2004 May	Street protests by opposition groups demanding a return to democracy. Royalist Prime Minister Surya Bahadur Thapa quits.
2004 June	King Gyanendra reappoints Sher Bahadur Deuba Prime Minister.
2005 February	King Gyanendra dismisses Prime Minister Deuba; assumes direct control of the executive and declares a state of emergency, citing the need to defeat Maoist rebels.
2005 November	Seven Party Alliance and the Maoists sign 12-point understanding in New Delhi to unseat 'autocratic monarchy'.
2006 April	King Gyanendra agrees to reinstate parliament following weeks of violent strikes and protests against direct royal rule; Girija Prasad Koirala appointed Prime Minister in Seven Party Alliance government; Maoist rebels call a three-month ceasefire.
2006 May	Parliament votes unanimously to curb the king's political powers; brings Nepal Army under civilian control; declares Nepal a secular state; the government holds peace talks with the Maoist rebels.

2006 June — Maoist Chairman Prachanda surfaces in Kathmandu for peace talks

2006 November — The government sign a peace deal with the Maoists – the Comprehensive Peace Agreement (CPA) – formally ending the decade-long insurgency.

2007 January — Interim Parliament constituted with Maoist participation; Interim constitution replaces 1990 constitution; Violent protests sweep Tarai; United Nations Mission in Nepal arrives.

2007 February — 'Federalism' inserted into constitutional text to appease Madhesi.

2007 April — Maoists join an interim government under Koirala, a move which brings them into the political mainstream.

2007 September — Maoists quit the interim government, demanding the abolition of the monarchy; November's constituent assembly elections are postponed; Nepali Congress reunites.

2007 December — Parliament approves the abolition of monarchy as part of peace deal with Maoists, who agree to rejoin government.

2008 January — A series of bomb blasts kill and injure dozens in

	the southern Terai plains, where activists have been demanding regional autonomy.
2008 February	Second Madhesi movement sweeps Terai.
2008 April	Former Maoist rebels win the largest bloc of seats in elections to the new Constituent Assembly (CA), but fail to achieve an outright majority.
2008 May	Nepal becomes a republic.
2008 June	King Gyanendra hands in crown and sceptre to government; vacates Narayanhity Palace
2008 July	Ram Baran Yadav becomes Nepal's first president.
2008 August	Maoist leader Pushpa Kamal Dahal aka Prachanda forms coalition government, with Nepali Congress going into opposition.
2009 May	Prachanda fails in his bid to replace army chief; resigns as Prime Minister; Madhav Kumar Nepal, CPN-UML, appointed Prime Minister in coalition with Nepali Congress.
2010 March	Former Prime Minister Girija Prasad Koirala, Nepali Congress, passes away, aged 85.

2010 May	The Constituent Assembly (CA) votes to extend the deadline for drafting the constitution, the first of four extensions.
2011 January	UNMIN ceases operations in Nepal.
2011 February	Madhav Kumar Nepal replaced as Prime Minister by Jhal Nath Khanal, also CPN-UML, in coalition with the Maoists.
2011 May	CA's extended life expires; gives itself another three months.
2011 August	Jhal Nath Khanal steps down; Baburam Bhattarai, CPN-Maoist, appointed Prime Minister.
2012 May	Supreme Court rules against further CA extension; The CA is dissolved after failing to produce a draft constitution. Prime Minister Bhattarai calls fresh CA elections for November 21.
2012 June	Nepali Congress and CPN-UML refuse participation in Maoist-supervised elections.
2013 March	Bhattarai steps down; Interim Election Government formed under Chief Justice Khil Raj Regmi; retired senior bureaucrats head key ministries.

2013 November — The Nepali Congress wins the second Constituent Assembly elections, pushing the former ruling Maoists into third place and leaving no party with a majority.

2014 February — Nepali Congress leader Sushil Koirala is elected prime minister after securing parliamentary support.

2014 August — Narendra Modi visits Nepal, first Indian Prime Minister in 17 years

2014 November — Nepal and India sign a deal to build a $1bn hydropower plant on Nepal's Arun river to counter crippling energy shortages.

2015 April — A 7.8-magnitude earthquake strikes Kathmandu and its surrounding areas killing more than 8,000 people, causing mass devastation and leaving millions homeless.

2015 June — 24 nations and international organisations pledge over US$4 billion in post-earthquake reconstruction assistance.

2015 August — Third Madhesi movement sweeps Terai; claims 50 lives.

2015 September — Parliament passes a landmark constitution, which defines Nepal as a secular country,

	despite calls to delay voting after more than 40 people are killed in protests.
2015 October	K.P. Sharma Oli, CPN-UML, appointed Prime Minister in coalition with CPN-Maoist Centre.
2016 February	Government lifts fuel rationing after the ethnic minority Madhesi communities, partially backed by India, end a six-month border blockade in protest over the new constitution which they say is discriminatory.
2016 February	Former Prime Minister Sushil Koirala, Nepali Congress, passes away, aged 77
2016 March	Prime Minister Oli initials landmark transit protocol with China
2016 July	Maoist party pulls out of the governing coalition. Prime Minister K.P. Oli resigns ahead of a no-confidence vote in parliament.
2016 August	Parliament elects former communist rebel leader and Maoist party leader Pushpa Kamal Dahal aka Prachanda as prime minister for the second time.
2017 April	China and Nepal hold their first ever joint military exercise.
2017 June	Pushpa Kamal Dahal replaced as prime minister

	by Nepali Congress leader Sher Bahadur Deuba under a rotation agreement reached the previous April and set to last until elections in February 2018.
2017 October	CPN-UML, CPN-Maoist Centre and Naya Shakti Party declare electoral alliance and future party merger; Baburam Bhattarai's Naya Shakti Party withdraws from the communist alliance.
2017 November	Parliamentary elections held under new constitution.
2017 December	Communist alliance sweeps polls.
2018 February	KP Sharma Oli sworn in as first Prime Minister of Federal Republic of Nepal.
2018 April	Prime Minister Oli visits India.
2018 May	CPN-UML and CPN-Maoist Centre merge; form Nepal Communist Party, the largest communist party in South Asia and third largest in Asia; Indian Prime Minister Narendra Modi visits Nepal.
2018 June	Prime Minister Oli visits China.
2018 August	Nepal hosts BIMSTEC summit.

2018 December — Foreign Minister Pradeep Gyawali visits Washington DC for talks with Secretary of State Mike Pompeo, marking a resumption of high-level contacts after 17 years.

2019 January — Prime Minister Oli becomes first Nepalese leader to address Davos Forum in Switzerland.

2019 April — President Bidya Bhandari visits China.

2019 June — Prime Minister Oli attends Narendra Modi's swearing in ceremony for a second term in New Delhi.

2019 October — President Xi Jinping visits Nepal, the first Chinese head of state to do so in 23 years.

2019 November — Protests erupt in Nepal after India releases new political map after reorganizing Jammu and Kashmir state.

2020 May — India inaugurates road link via Lipulekh to Kailash Mansarovar in Tibet through territory Nepal claims. Nepal issues new political map incorporating territories it claims India has been occupying; Oli claims coronavirus strain from India is more dangerous than the original Chinese variant.

2020 June — Parliament adopts constitutional amendment

updating the map in the national emblem; Oli accuses India of plotting to remove him from office.

2020 July

Oli claims Lord Ram was born in Nepal and accused India of cultural encroachment; India-Nepal media war escalates. As rifts in ruling NCP widen over demands that Oli relinquish either the premiership or the party presidency, Chinese ambassador Hou Yanqi steps up mediation efforts.

2020 August

Nepal and India resume official contacts after months.

Dramatis Personae

Ai Ping: Senior Chinese Communist Party official instrumental in devising Beijing's early post-monarchy policy on Nepal and the Maoists.

Baidya, Mohan: One-time mentor of Maoist supremo Pushpa Kamal Dahal, he broke away from the party accusing it ideological deviation to form his own revolutionary faction in 2012.

Bhandari, Bidya: President of Nepal since 2015. Widow of CPN-UML general secretary Madan Bhandari.

Bhandari, Madan: Charismatic general secretary of Nepal Communist Party (Unified Marxist-Leninist) who died in a car accident in 1993.

Bhattarai, Baburam: Prime Minister of Nepal from August 2011 to March 2013. Chief ideologue and second in command of the Nepal Communist Party (Maoist), he severed ties with the party in 2015.

'Biplab' (Netra Bikram Chand): A leading member of the insurgency-era Maoist party, he broke away to form his own party to continue fighting for a communist state.

Dahal, Pushpa Kamal: Chairman of Communist Party of Nepal (Maoist), he emerged in public in 2006 after spending decades underground, including during the bloody 10-year 'people's war'. Elected prime minister in 2008, he resigned after President reversed his order sacking the army chief. He returned to the premiership from August 2016 to June 2017. He is co-chair of the ruling Nepal Communist Party since his party merged with the CPN-UML in 2018.

Dalai Lama: Spiritual leader of the Tibetans and Nobel Peace Prize laureate who has been lives in exile in India since fleeing his homeland in 1959.

Deuba, Sher Bahadur: Four-time premier, he headed the governments King Gyanendra sacked in October 2002 and February 2005. He had broken away from the Nepali Congress to form his own faction in 2002, which reunited in 2007. Deuba had headed a coalition government in 1995-1996 and returned as prime minister in 2017-2018. He is the president of the main opposition Nepali Congress.

Doval, Ajit: National Security Adviser to Prime Minister Narendra Modi since 2014, he retired as director of India's Intelligence Bureau in 2005.

Gachhadar, Bijay Kumar: Nepali Congress leader who quit the party to join the Madhesi Janadhikar Forum in 2008. He served as deputy prime minister in several coalition governments. In 2017, Gachhadar merged his Madhesi Democratic Forum with the Nepali Congress.

Gajurel, Chandra Prakash: Senior insurgency-era Maoist leader who broke away with Mohan Baidya in 2012 to form a revolutionary faction.

Gandhi, Indira: Former prime minister of India who continued her father Jawaharlal Nehru's policy of quiet engagement with the Nepalese monarchy until her assassination in 1984.

Gandhi, Rajiv: Prime minister of India in the latter half of the 1980s, during which Indo-Nepalese relations sunk to one of their worst levels. He was assassinated in 1991.

Gandhi, Sonia: Widow of Rajiv Gandhi and president of the Congress party.

Gautam, Bam Dev: A leader of the CPN-UML, he served as deputy prime minister in the first Maoist-led government in 2008-2009. He is a senior leader of the ruling Nepal Communist Party.

Gyawali, Pradeep: CPN-UML leader, Gyawali is Foreign Minister of Nepal since 2018.

Hou Yanqi: China's ambassador to Nepal since 2018.

Hu Jintao: President of China from 2003 to 2013.

Jaishankar, S.: Indian External Affairs Minister since 2019. As Foreign Secretary in 2015, he unsuccessfully pressed Nepalese leaders to seek broad-based consultations with marginalized groups before promulgating the new constitution. The new constitution triggered massive protests and worsened Nepal-India relations.

Jiang Zemin: President of China from 1989 to 2003, who visited Nepal in 1996.

Karmapa Lama: Third-ranking Tibetan spiritual leader who fled China to India via Nepal in 2000.

Katawal, Rookmangud: Chief of Nepal Army from 2006-2009, during whose tenure the military distanced itself from the monarchy before its abolition in 2008. After failing to dismiss from office him the following year, the Maoist government resigned.

Khanal, Jhal Nath: Prime Minister of Nepal from February to August 2011.

Koirala, Bisweshwar Prasad: Nepal's first elected premier, he was ousted by King Mahendra in December 1960. After spending eight years in a Kathmandu prison, Koirala went into exile in India and led his Nepali Congress in opposition to the palace. Returning to Nepal in 1976 with a programme of national reconciliation with the monarchy, he died six years later.

Koirala, Girija Prasad: Nepal's second elected prime minister in 1991, he became premier two more times before King Gyanendra's takeover. In April 2007 returned to power heading a coalition of opposition parties and former Maoist rebels as part of a peace process. He died in 2010.

Koirala, Sushil: Prime Minister of Nepal from February 2014 to

October 2015 and Nepali Congress President from 2010 until his death in 2016.

Koshyari, Bhagat Singh: Senior BJP leader and co-chair of the Eminent Persons Group on reviewing bilateral relations. He was later appointed governor of Maharashtra state.

Kwatra, Vinay Mohan: Indian ambassador to Nepal since 2020.

Li Keqiang: Prime Minister of China since 2013.

Li Peng: Premier of China from 1988 to 1998. Visited Nepal in 1989.

Li Zhaoxing: Foreign Minister of China who visited Kathmandu after King Gyanendra's takeover in 2005.

Mahara, Krishna Bahadur: Speaker of Nepal's parliament from 2017 to 2019, he was a key insurgency-era Maoist interlocutor with the government in 2001 and 2003-2004. He served as deputy prime minister in several coalition governments.

Mao Zedong: Founder of the People's Republic of China, who shared close ties with the Nepalese monarchy. Two decades after his death in 1976, Nepalese followers began a bloody insurgency aimed at abolishing the monarchy.

Menon, Shiv Shankar: Former foreign secretary and national security adviser of India who dealt with Nepal during critical phases of the peace process.

Modi, Narendra: Prime Minister of India since 2014.

Moriarty, James F.: U.S. ambassador in Kathmandu from 2004 to 2007.

Mukherjee, Pranab: President of India from 2012-2017. As senior minister under several Congress government, he dealt with Nepal extensively over five decades, including during the 2005-2006 effort to bring the Maoists and mainstream parties together.

Mukherjee, Shiv Shankar: India's ambassador to Nepal from 2004 t0 2008, during King Gyanendra's takeover and fall.

Nehru, Jawaharlal: India's first prime minister who mediated the Delhi Compromise of 1951, which replaced Nepal's century-old Rana regime with a multiparty system under the monarchy.

Nepal, Madhav Kumar: Prime Minister of Nepal from 2009 to 2011, he was general secretary of the CPN-UML from 1993 to 2008.

Oli, Khadga Prasad Sharma: Prime Minister of Nepal since October 2018. Co-chair of the Nepal Communist Party, he also served as premier from 2015 to 2016.

Pompeo, Mike: US Secretary of State since April 2018.

Powell, Colin: US Secretary of State from 2001 to 2005, he paid a visited Nepal in 2002.

Puri, Manjeev Singh: Indian ambassador to Nepal from 2017 to 2020.

Prachanda: see Dahal, Pushpa Kamal.

Prasad, Jayant: Indian ambassador to Nepal from 2011 to 2013.

Qiu Guohong: Chinese ambassador to Nepal from 2008 to 2001.

Rae, Ranjit: Indian ambassador to Nepal from 2013 to 2017.

Rana, Mohan Shamsher: The last Rana prime minister, he held power from 1948 to 1951. After the Delhi Compromise, he led a coalition government with the Nepali Congress, which collapsed nine months later. Shortly thereafter, he went into exile in Bangalore, where he died in 1965.

Rao, P.V. Narasimha: Prime Minister of India from 1991-1996, he dealt with Nepal extensively also during his earlier capacity as foreign minister.

Raut, C.K.: Chief of Janamat Party, formed in 2019 after he signed an 11-point agreement with the government ending his separatist movement in the Terai.

Regmi, Khil Raj: Chairman of cabinet of technocrats that served from March 2013 to February 2014 to hold elections to Nepal's second constituent assembly.

Saran, Shyam: Indian ambassador to Nepal from 2002 to 2005, he went on to become Indian Foreign Secretary (2004-2006). Actively involved in creating the alliance between the Maoists and mainstream parties, he continued visiting Nepal as an envoy of the Indian prime minister.

Shah, Aishwarya: Queen who was killed in the 2001 palace massacre.

Shah, Birendra Bir Bikram: King who was killed in the 2001 palace massacre.

Shah, Dhirendra: Youngest brother of King Birendra, he was stripped of his royal title and privileges. He returned to Nepal after several years of self-exile and was in preliminary talks with the Maoist rebels. He was killed in the 2001 palace massacre.

Shah, Dipendra: Crown prince, who was declared king for two days while in a coma. He allegedly killed his parents, siblings and other royal relatives on the night of June 1, 2001 before turning the gun on himself.

Shah, Gyanendra Bir Bikram: Second son of King Mahendra, he briefly sat on the throne in 1951 after his grandfather, King Tribhuvan, led the rest of the royal family into exile in India. He ascended to the throne a second time after his brother, King Birendra, and the immediate royal family perished in the 2001 palace massacre. He was sidelined after the April 2006 uprising and became a commoner in 2008 when the elected constituent assembly formally abolished the monarchy.

Shah, Himani: Wife of former crown prince Paras Shah and daughter in law of ex-monarch Gyanendra Shah, she is the mother of Hridayendra Shah.

Shah, Hridayendra: Grandson of ex-king Gyanendra and son of ex-crown prince Paras, born in 2002, some see him becoming a ceremonial king under a restored monarchy.

Shah, Komal: Queen of Nepal, she survived the 2001 palace massacre with gunshot wounds.

Shah, Mahendra. King from 1955 to 1972, castigated for destroying Nepalese democracy but credited with strengthening the country's independence and international profile.

Shah, Paras: The only son of e-king Gyanendra, he has been dogged by a series of controversies predating his elevation as crown prince between 2001 and 2006.

Shah, Prithvi Narayan: King of Gorkha who captured Kathmandu Valley in 1769 and turned it into the capital of what would go on to become modern Nepal. He died in 1775.

Shah, Ratna: Queen of King Mahendra and the senior-most ex-royal.

Shah, Tribhuvan Bir Bikram: Monarch who, through the 1951 Delhi Compromise, regained political powers the palace had lost to the Ranas over a century earlier. He died in 1955.

Shrestha, Narayan Kaji: Senior leader and spokesperson of the ruling Nepal Communist Party who comes from the Maoist stream. A member of the upper house of parliament, Shrestha has served as deputy prime minister.

Shringla, Harsh Vardhan: India's Foreign Secretary since 2020.

Singh, Jaswant: Foreign and finance and defence minister in Bharatiya Janata Party-led governments in 1996 and 1998-2004, who dealt regularly with Nepal.

Singh, Karan: Former regent of Kashmir and Congress leader, he arrived as Prime Minister Manmohan Singh's special emissary to King Gyanendra in April 2006 during the height of the anti-palace movement.

Singh, Manmohan: Prime Minister of India from 2004 to 2014 representing the Congress party.

Singh, Natwar: Former Foreign Minister of India under Congress governments, who dealt with extensively with Nepal.

Singh, Ramraja Prasad: An early campaigner for a republic in Nepal, he was the Maoists' first candidate for president in 2008.

Sood, Rakesh: Indian ambassador to Nepal from 2008 to 2011.

Swaraj, Sushma: Indian Foreign Minister from 2014 to 2019.

Tang Jiaxuan: Former Chinese foreign minister and state councillor and last Chinese official to deal directly with the Nepalese monarchy in March 2006.

Thapa, Bhek Bahadur: Former foreign and finance minister and co-chair of the Eminent Persons Group established to review Nepal-India bilateral relations.

Thapa, Kamal: Leader of the Rastriya Prajatantra Party, the only major party still supporting the monarchy, he served as deputy prime minister from 2005 to 2016 and from 2017 and 2018 in coalition governments.

Thapa, Pyar Jung: Army chief during King Gyanendra's 2005-2006 direct rule, he was reported to have played a major role in opening dialogue between the palace and the Seven Party Alliance.

Thapa, Ram Bahadur: Home Minister since 2018, he was a senior Maoist commander during the 1996-2006 'people's war'.

Vajpayee, Atal Behari: Prime Minister of India in 1996 and then from 1998 to 2004.

Wang Yi: Chinese Foreign Minister since 2013, he has visited Nepal several times.

Wen Jiabao: Premier of China from 2003 to 2013, who visited Nepal in 2012.

Wu Chuntai: Chinese ambassador to Nepal from 2013-2016.

Xi Jinping: President of China since 2013, who visited Nepal in 2019.

Yadav, Ram Baran: First President of Federal Republic of Nepal, who served from 2008 to 2013.

Yadav, Upendra: Former deputy prime minister under several

governments. A former Maoist, he founded the Madhesi Janadhikar Forum in 2007 and has been a leading campaigner for indigenous rights.

Yang Houlan: Chinese ambassador to Nepal from 2011 to 2013.

Yang Jiechi: China's Foreign Minister since 2007-2013.

Yechury, Sitaram: Communist Party of India-Marxist leader who played a key role in forming the alliance between Nepal's Maoists and mainstream political parties.

Yu Hong: Chinese ambassador to Nepal from 2016 to 2018.

Zhou Enlai: Premier of China from 1949 until his death in 1976.

Zhou Yongkang: Member of the Chinese Communist Party's 17th Politburo Standing Committee between 2007 and 2012, who visited Nepal in 2011. He was convicted of corruption-related charges in 2014 and expelled from the party.

Zhu Rongji: Premier of China from 1998 to 2003, who visited Nepal in 2001.

Bibliography

Adhikari, Aditya. 2014. The Bullet and the Ballot Box: The Story of Nepal's Maoist Revolution. New York and London: Verso.

Aggarwal, Prachi. 2020. 'Wuhan Spirit and Modi-Xi Dynamics'. In One Mountain Two Tigers: India, China and the High Himalayas, edited by Shakti Sinha. New Delhi: Pentagon Press. pp.167-182.

Bhattarai, Kamal Dev. 2020. "China's silence adds to Nepal's woes on Lipulekh". Annapurna Express. May 18, 2020. Retrieved from: https://theannapurnaexpress.com/news/chinas-silence-adds-to-nepals-woes-on-lipulekh-2497.

Bhattarai, Kamal Dev. 2019. 'China-India Plus: Is it in Nepal's interest?'. Annapurna Express. November 3, 2019. Retrieved from: https://theannapurnaexpress.com/news/china-india-plus-is-it-in-nepals-interest-1987.

Bhattarai, Kamal Dev. 2018. 'Between Two Giants: Why and India-China Dialogue Mechanism Benefits Nepal'. South Asian Voices.

November 13, 2018. Retrieved from: https://southasianvoices.org/ between-two-giants-india-china-dialogue-mechanism-benefits- nepal/.

Dixit, Kunda. 2010. 'A New Himalayan Game', Fletcher Forum of World Affairs, Vol. 34, No. 1, Winter.

Fairbank, John K. 1968. The Chinese World Order: Traditional China's Foreign Relations. Cambridge: Harvard University Press.

Garver, John W. 2001. Protracted Contest: Sino-Indian Rivalry in the Twentieth Century. Seattle and London: University of Washington Press.

Gautam, Kul Chandra. 2015. "U.N.'s Mixed Messages on Nepal's Constitution". Inter Press Service. September 28, 2015. Retrieved from: http://www.ipsnews.net/2015/09/opinion-u-n-s-mixed- messages-on-nepals-constitution/.

Ghosh, Rudroneel. 2017. "Nepal PM's Visit: Kathmandu can be an interlocutor between New Delhi and Beijing". Talking Turkey. The Times of India Blogs. August 19, 2017. Retrieved from: https:// blogs.indiatimes.com/talkingturkey/nepal-pms-visit-kathmandu- can-be-an-interlocutor-between-new-delhi-and-beijing/.

Ghoshal, Antara Singh. 2020. "The Standoff and China's India Policy Dilemma" The Hindu. July 15, 2020. Retrieved from: https:// www.thehindu.com/opinion/lead/the-stand-off-andchinas-india- policy-dilemma/article32083539.ece.

Gupta, Arvind. 2010. 'India needs a new paradigm in its Nepal policy', IDSA Comment. August 18, 2010. Retrieved from: www. idsa.in/idsacomments/IndianeedsanewparadigminitsNepalpolicy_agupta_180810.

Hou Yanqi. 2020. "An interview with Chinese ambassador to Nepal Hou Yanqi". Annapurna Express. August 30, 2020. Retrieved from: https://theannapurnaexpress.com/news/an-interview-with-chinese-ambassador-hou-yanqi-2751.

Hsiao, Russell. 2008. Nepal Following China's Economic Path. China Brief 8:14. Washington DC: Jamestown Foundation. July 3, 2008. Retrieved from: https://jamestown.org/program/nepal-following-chinas-economic-path/

Hu Shisheng. 2017. "Trans-Himalayan Handshake". The Kathmandu Post. August 17, 2017. Retrieved from: https://kathmandupost.com/opinion/2017/08/17/trans-himalayan-handshake.

Hu Shisheng. 2015. 'Nepal most viable bridge between China and South Asia'. Interview. The Kathmandu Post. October 12, 2015. Retrieved from: https://kathmandupost.com/interviews/2015/10/12/nepal-most-viable-bridge-between-china-and-south-asia

Hu Weijia. 2017. "India shouldn't see Nepal's economy as a strategic battlefield against China's influence". Global Times. August 23, 2017. Retrieved from: https://www.globaltimes.cn/content/1062835.shtml.

Huang Ge. 2019. "Chinese envoy slams US official over BRI criticism in Nepal". Global Times. February 26, 2019. Retrieved from: https://www.globaltimes.cn/content/1140259.shtml

Indian Express. 2018. 'No Zero Sum Game'. Editorial. June 25, 2018. Retrieved from: https://indianexpress.com/article/opinion/editorials/no-zero-sum-game-pm-narendra-modi-kp-sharma-oli-india-nepal-relations-5231779/.

International Crisis Group (ICG). 2016. 'Nepal's Divisive New Constitution: An Existential Crisis'. 2016. Asia Report N°276. Brussels. April 4, 2016. Retrieved from: https://www.crisisgroup.org/asia/south-asia/nepal/nepal's-divisive-new-constitution-existential-crisis.

Jaishankar, S. 2020. The India Way: Strategies for an Uncertain World. Noida, Uttar Pradesh: HarperCollins Publishers India.

Jaiswal, Pramod. 2020. "India-China Rivalry in Nepal". In Navigating India-China Rivalry: Perspectives from South Asia, edited by C Raja Mohan and Chan Jia. Institute of South Asian Studies. National University of Singapore. pp-49-56. Retrieved from: https://www.isas.nus.edu.sg/papers/managing-india-china-rivalry-perspectives-from-south-asia/.

Jha, Prashant. 2014. Battle of the New Republic: A Contemporary History of Nepal. New Delhi: Aleph.

Jha, Prashant. 2012 'A Nepali Perspective on International

Involvement in Nepal'. In Nepal in Transition: From People's War to Fragile Peace, edited by Sebastian von Einsiedel, David M. Malone, and Suman Pradhan. London: Cambridge University Press. pp.333-358.

Josse, M.R. 2020. 'Nepal: A Sino-Indian condominium?' Peoples Review Weekly. Kathmandu. August 24, 2020. Retrieved from: https://www.peoplesreview.com.np/2020/08/24/nepal-a-sino-indian-condominium/

Katawal, Rookmangud. 2014. Atmakatha [An Autobiography]. 1st ed. Kathmandu: Nepalaya.

Koirala, Bhaskar. 2011. 'Sino-Nepalese Relations: Factoring in India'. China Report. 46:3: pp.231-242

Lovell, Julia. 2019. Maoism: A Global History. New York: Vintage Books.

Madan, Tanvi. 2020. Fateful Triangle: How China Shaped U.S.-India Relations During the Cold War. Washington DC: Brookings Institution Press.

Mishra, Rabindra. 2004. "India's Role in Nepal's Maoist Insurgency." Asian Survey. Vol. 44, No. 5. September-October 2004, pp.627-646

Muni, S.D. 2020. "India Meets China in its Periphery". In Navigating India-China Rivalry: Perspectives from South Asia, edited by C Raja Mohan and Chan Jia. Institute of South Asian Studies. National University of Singapore. pp-89-98.

Retrieved from: https://www.isas.nus.edu.sg/papers/managing-india-china-rivalry-perspectives-from-south-asia/.

Muni, S.D. 2012. "Bringing the Maoists down from the Hills: India's Role". In Nepal in Transition: From People's War to Fragile Peace, edited by Sebastian von Einsiedel, David M. Malone, and Suman Pradhan. London: Cambridge University Press. pp.313-331.

Nayak, Nihar. 2007. "The Maoist Movement in Nepal and Its Tactical Digressions: A Study of Strategic Revolutionary Phases, and Future Implications," Strategic Analysis, 31:6, 915-942.

Pande, Aparna. 2020. Making India Great: The Promise of a Reluctant Global Power. New Delhi: HarperCollins Publishers India.

Pandey, Ramesh Nath. 2015. Kutniti Ra Rajniti [Diplomacy and Politics]: An Autobiography. Kathmandu: Sangri-La Books.

Ramachandran, Sudha. 2020. India's "Tibet Card" in the Stand-Off with China:
More Provocative than Productive. China Brief: 20:17. The Jamestown Foundation. Retrieved from: https://jamestown.org/program/indias-tibet-card-in-the-stand-off-with-china-more-provocative-than-productive/.

Ren Yuanzhe and Wu Lin. 2020. "Implications of India's Indo-Pacific Strategy on China-India Relations: A Chinese Perspective". In Navigating India-China Rivalry: Perspectives from South Asia, edited by C Raja Mohan and Chan Jia. Institute of South Asian Studies. National University of Singapore. pp-79-88.
Retrieved from: https://www.isas.nus.edu.sg/papers/managing-

india-china-rivalry-perspectives-from-south-asia/.

Rolland, Nadège (Editor). 2020. An Emerging China-Centric Order: China's Vision for a New World Order in Practice. The National Bureau of Asian Research. NBR Special Report #87. August 2020. Retrieved from: https://www.nbr.org/publication/an-emerging-china-centric-order-chinas-vision-for-a-new-world-order-in-practice/.

'Royal takeover not behind India skipping 2005 SAARC Summit'. 2011. EKantipur.com. April 1, 2011. Retrieved from https://advance.lexis.com/api/document?collection=news&id=urn:contentItem:52HJ-0JW1-F12F-F4WS-00000-00&context=1516831.

Saran, Shyam. 2017. How India Sees the World: Kautilya to the 21st Century. New Delhi: Juggernaut Books.

Shah, Vivek Kumar. 2010. Maile Dekheko Durbar [Witnessing Palace, Power and Politics Memoirs of a Military Secretary of the King of Nepal]. Kathmandu: Yeti Publications.

Sharma, Sudheer. 2019. The Nepal Nexus: An Inside Account of the Maoists, the Durbar and New Delhi. New Delhi: Penguin India.

'Sikkim Standoff: What If We Enter Kalapani, Kashmir, China, Asks India'. 2017. Press Trust of India. Retrieved from: https://www.bloombergquint.com/politics/sikkim-standoff-what-if-we-enter-kalapani-kashmir-china-asks-india.

Sikri, Rajiv. 2006. Challenge and Strategy: Rethinking India's

Foreign Policy. New Delhi: Sage.

Subramanian, Nirupama. 2011. "Why India Stopped 2005 SAARC Summit". The Hindu. March 29, 2011. Retrieved from: https://www.thehindu.com/news/the-india-cables/Why-India-stopped-2005-Dhaka-SAARC-summit/article14965642.ece.

Suhrke, Astri. 2011. "Virtues of a Narrow Mission: The UN Peace Operation in Nepal. Global Governance: 17, 37–55.

Thapa, Deepak and Alexander Ramsbotham (Editors). 2017. "Two steps forward, one step back:
The Nepal peace process". London: Conciliation Resources. March 2017. Retrieved from: https://www.c-r.org/accord/nepal.

Upadhya, Rajib. 2020. Cabals and Cartels: An Up Close Look at Nepal's Turbulent Transition and Disrupted Development. Kathmandu: FinePrint.

Upadhya, Sanjay. 2008. The Raj Lives: India in Nepal. New Delhi: Vitasta.

Upadhya, Sanjay. 2012. Nepal and the Geo-Strategic Rivalry Between China and India. London and New York: Routledge.

Wang Hongwei, "Chin Chup Lagera Basdaina" [China Won't Sit Silently By], Nepal, November 4, 2007.

"Whether To Accept The US Government's Grants Lies Within Nepal: Chinese ambassador Hou Yanqi". 2020. New

Spotlight Online. January 3, 2020. Retrieved from: https://www.spotlightnepal.com/2020/01/03/whether-accept-us-governments-grants-lies-within-nepal-chinese-ambassador-hou-yanqi/.

Xu Liang. 2016. "Nepal risks missing chance with China". Global Times. August 19, 2016. Retrieved from: http://www.globaltimes.cn/content/1007091.shtml.

Zhang Li. 2006. "Conflict Management and Nation-building in Nepal: China's Perspective and Interest Calculus." Paper presented at the Conference on Globalization and Peace Building, organised by the Swedish Network of Peace, Conflict & Development Research, at Uppsala, November 6-8, 2006. Retrieved from: http://www.peacenetwork.se/documents_publications/Zhang_Li.pdf.

Zhao Gancheng. 2010. "South Asia's Position in the International Order and Choice Before China", South Asian Studies (Chinese), No.1.

Index

Buddha 34, 100

Buddhism 86

Bush, George W. 44, 146

C

Calcutta 152, 194

Cameron, David 119

Carter, Jimmy 44

Central Intelligence Agency 6, 46, 101

Chang Wanquan 130

Chen Bingde 83

Chen Fengxian 112

China , 2, 3, 4, 5, 6, 7, 8, 9, 10, 11, 12, 13, 14, 21, 24, 26, 27, 32, 33, 37, 38, 44, 45, 46, 52, 53, 54, 55, 56, 61, 62, 64, 65, 66, 67, 68, 69, 70, 71, 75, 80, 83, 84, 85, 87, 90, 91, 99, 100, 101, 102, 104, 105, 106, 107, 108, 111, 113, 118, 119, 120, 121, 122, 123, 124, 125, 126, 127, 128, 129, 131, 132, 133, 134, 136, 138, 139, 140, 141, 142, 145, 146, 147, 150, 152, 154, 155, 156, 157, 158, 159, 161, 162, 166, 167, 169, 170, 173, 174, 175, 176, 177, 179, 180, 181, 182, 183, 187, 188, 190, 191, 192, 195, 196, 197, 198, 199, 200, 201, 202, 203, 204, 205, 206, 207, 208, 210, 211, 212, 213, 214, 215, 216, 217, 220, 222, 224, 226, 228, 241, 242, 243, 247, 248, 249, 255, 256, 257, 258, 259, 260, 261, 262, 263, 264, 265, 268, 270, 271, 272, 274

and aid to Nepal 80, 86, 90, 100, 101, 102, 105, 106, 107, 122, 131, 134, 142, 150

and earthquake aid 107, 180

and federalism 67, 68, 75, 91, 92, 102

and India 3, 5, 7, 12, 14, 37, 46, 52, 62, 68, 71, 79, 80, 99, 100, 104, 107, 120, 122, 124, 125, 126, 128, 131, 132, 133, 135, 139, 142, 154, 180, 199, 201, 202, 203, 204, 205, 206, 211

and Maoists 1, 4, 5, 6, 14, 46, 47, 52, 56, 61, 64, 65, 66, 67, 70, 79, 99, 100, 113, 129, 177, 202

and monarchy 1, 3, 4, 6, 7, 9, 11, 12, 13, 14, 61, 68, 69, 155, 162, 166, 169, 174, 179, 203

and Nepal Army 64, 83, 84

and Terai 62, 123

and Tibet 69, 71, 80, 83, 84, 86, 89, 92, 100, 101, 105, 155, 173, 210

and United Nations 53

and United States 6, 12, 14, 44, 46, 72, 99, 146, 161, 163, 198, 199, 204

and UNMIN 32, 33, 80, 207

China card 11, 120, 121, 175

China-Nepal-India Economic Corridor 108, 140

Chinese Communist Party 68, 86

Chinese People's Liberation Army